OLD TOWN ROAD

SINGLES ▲ A SERIES EDITED BY JOSHUA CLOVER AND EMILY J. LORDI

OLD TOWN ROAD

CHRIS MOLANPHY

DUKE UNIVERSITY PRESS DURHAM AND LONDON 2023

Project Editor: Jessica Ryan
Designed by Matthew Tauch
Typeset in Bitter and Work Sans by Copperline Book Services

Library of Congress Cataloging-in-Publication Data
Names: Molanphy, Chris, author.
Title: Old town road / Chris Molanphy.
Other titles: Singles.
Description: Durham : Duke University Press, 2023. | Series:
Singles | Includes bibliographical references and index.
Identifiers: LCCN 2023008300 (print)
LCCN 2023008301 (ebook)
ISBN 9781478025511 (paperback)
ISBN 9781478020738 (hardcover)
ISBN 9781478027645 (ebook)
Subjects: LCSH: Lil Nas X, 1999–Criticism and interpretation. |
Old town road (Song) | Rap (Music)—History and criticism. | Popular
music—United States—2011–2020. | BISAC: MUSIC / General
Classification: LCC ML420.L5725 M635 2023 (print) |
LCC ML420.L5725 (ebook) |
DDC 782.421649–dc23/eng/20230613
LC record available at https://lccn.loc.gov/2023008300
LC ebook record available at https://lccn.loc.gov/2023008301

For Anna and Loki

CONTENTS

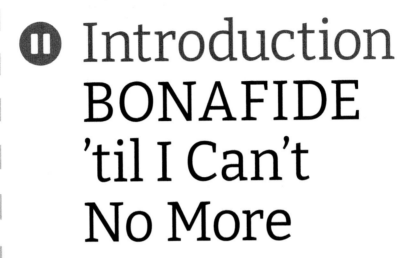

Introduction
BONAFIDE 'til I Can't No More

"Old Town Road" as the Endpoint of a Century of Genre and Chart Evolution

THE LAST DAY OF THE SCHOOL YEAR at Lander Elementary in Mayfield Heights, Ohio, was Wednesday, May 29, 2019. Five days earlier, the fifth graders had taken part in the school's annual talent show, capping off the day with a schoolwide performance of the No. 1 song in America. When video of that adorable performance got back to the artist behind the original song, he decided to visit

Mayfield Heights and surprise the kids, just before summer, with an in-person performance of his hit, live in their gymnasium. The performer—a southern Black twenty-year-old born Montero Lamar Hill—arrived in his now-standard uniform of cowboy hat, boots, and fringed jacket. Hill adjusted his outfit and was escorted by the school principal into the gym.

And the kids lost their damn minds.

As the young man who had dubbed himself Lil Nas X began singing "Old Town Road" on the gym's makeshift stage, the Lander Elementary kids practically screamed the lyrics back at him, including the titter-worthy line about "bull-ridin' and boobies."

Minutes before stepping out onstage to this frenzied reception, the twenty-year-old told a camera, "I'm finna do the biggest show of my life." He was only half kidding. As recently as four months earlier, Hill hadn't even been signed to a recording contract. Rapid rises to fame were becoming more commonplace in the post-YouTube, post-Spotify, early TikTok era of internet-fueled music virality. But even by those standards, Hill's trajectory seemed meteoric. As the young man himself told *Rolling Stone* just one month before his Lander Elementary performance, "Time's been going pretty fast."

....

"Old Town Road" was a singular phenomenon—a one of one. *New York Times* journalist Jazmine Hughes aptly calls it "an international anthem of defiance, tenacity and travel plans." Few songs have experienced its rapid and broad cultural penetration. Within months of its creation, it connected with grade-schoolers and grandparents, blue-staters and red-staters, the very online and the defiantly analog. It was heard in more than forty countries around the world. It was consumed by millions of fans of pop, R&B, rap, dance, rock, and, yes, also country music—some driven merely by curiosity, most because it's just a very catchy song.

In at least one key statistical sense, no song has done what "Old Town Road" did—as of this writing, it remains the longest-lasting No. 1 hit of all time on America's flagship pop chart, the *Billboard* Hot 100. Its nineteen weeks at No. 1 was more than twice as long as the Beatles' biggest hit, and more than the biggest hits by Michael Jackson and Madonna *combined*. And consider: those superstars' historic No. 1s (respectively: "Hey Jude," nine weeks at No. 1 in 1968; "Billie Jean," seven weeks, 1983; and "Take a Bow," seven weeks, 1995) were deployed years into each hitmaker's career. "Old Town Road" was Lil Nas X's first-ever charting single.

Chart historians like the author of this book make hay out of comparisons like these, with the tacit understanding that the music business of 1968 and that of 2019 were very different. While the Hot 100's underlying formula has remained broadly the same over its sixty-five years of existence, the chart behaves very differently today than it once did. So, yes: explaining how Lil Nas X pulled off his historic chart feat with "Old Town Road" means dissecting the chart as much as dissecting the song. Not unlike the home-run record of Babe Ruth's day versus Barry

Bonds's, we must reckon with the rules of the sport—and the performance-enhancers that warp those rules—as we weigh the players' feats.

Nonetheless, "Old Town Road" earned its climactic chart record. The song is an apotheosis, the culmination of a series of populist trends that had been building toward Lil Nas X's moment: trends in genre, in technology, in consumption, in identity. On his signature hit, Lil Nas X—whom I'll often reference as "Nas," his preferred nickname—simultaneously lionized and satirized genre tropes. In so doing, he troubled the very idea of genre: whether it is necessary or even relevant.

Nas's smash is a country song built out of an alternative rock sample, a hip-hop song in which nobody really raps, a comical song that somehow transcends novelty. It achieved all of this organically, using profoundly inorganic technologies. To the then-twenty-year-old Hill's generation, these technologies have become so commonplace that they are now the lingua franca of musical creation. It took advantage of changes in our pop metabolism—how memes form movements, a virality that is now reified by the hit parade. "Old Town Road" even qualifies as a queer anthem—and not only because Montero Hill picked Pride Month 2019, right in the middle of his epic chart-topping run, to come out of the closet.

In sum, "Old Town Road" summarizes the musical past, while pointing the way toward our cultural future. "But," you may be asking, "is it a great song?"

I'd argue that "Old Town Road" is an excellent pop song: sturdy, witty, inspired. But it's an even more amazing pop artifact. While listening to it, you can't help but think about its backstory, even if it's your first time hearing it. This only enhances its charms. Many great songs in pop history, at their core, revel in their own existence, from "Like a Rolling Stone" and "Stayin' Alive" to "Smells like Teen Spirit" and "Get Ur Freak On." They are, at a root level, about themselves. The self-consciousness of "Old Town Road" is one of many things that makes it great.

Charts, too, are reflexive and self-reinforcing. They are feedback loops that reflect popularity back at an industry eager to make things more popular, to turn once-cool things into commonplace things that are then replaced by the next cool thing. What makes charts exciting—the reason I focus on them in my writing, my podcast, and my scholarship—is that the industry rarely knows with any certainty what cool is. Truly unique songs are pop moments that reset our understanding of where cool lies.

"Old Town Road" was one of those—a pop moment that channeled decades of Americana and the bleeding edge of cool. All of which led up to those kids screaming at Lil Nas X about bull-riding and boobies in the Lander Elementary gym.

▶ 01 WIDE-EYED 'til I Can't No More

The Maker of "Old Town Road" and

the Elements of Its Creation

THE WEEK LIL NAS X WAS BORN, the No. 1 song on *Billboard*'s Hot 100, America's flagship pop chart, was "No Scrubs," a breezy, sassy track from Atlanta girl-group trio TLC. Format-wise, the song was pop, hip-hop, and R&B all at once—not unlike TLC themselves, who fused soul singing and fierce rapping with radio-friendly hooks and a DayGlo fashion sense. They were their own genre.

Lyrically, "No Scrubs" was basically a meme before the internet had latched onto that word. Written primarily by Kandi Burruss, a songwriter formerly of Xscape, another girl group, "No Scrubs" emerged practically fully formed: Burress took some doggerel she'd written about shiftless boyfriends—"scrubs"—and applied it to a prewritten backing track that producer Kevin "She'kspere" Briggs gave her to play in her car. The opening lines read like an *Urban Dictionary* definition: "A scrub is a guy who thinks he's fly / And is also known as a buster / Always talking 'bout what he wants / And just sits on his broke ass." It was a deliberate attempt to define a trend, and it worked. Everybody involved with TLC knew it had the makings of a smash. Executive producer Dallas Austin insisted "No Scrubs" should be the first single from their 1999 album *FanMail*. By the time it reached No. 1, the word *scrub* had entered the lexicon.

Atlanta origins, genre self-invention, meme-able lyrics applied to a precooked beat: All of this could also describe "Old Town Road." If you regard chart hits as astrological symbols, well . . . Nas was destined for this shit.

. . . .

Montero Lamar Hill was born in Atlanta on April 9, 1999, around the birth peak of Generation Z. Montero's mother named him for the Mitsubishi sport-utility vehicle of the same name. After his parents split at age six, Montero was raised, at first, by his mother and grandmother in the Bankhead Courts projects, which is steeped in Atlanta hip-hop lore. Bankhead spawned eventual twenty-first-century rap stars T.I., Young Dro, and D4L and was renowned for spawning its own dance, the Bankhead bounce, an infectious shoulder-shimmy codified by rappers L. "Diamond" Atkins and the Ying Yang Twins' D-Roc; the dance was popularized in music videos by Atlanta stars OutKast and TLC, and even adopted by Michael Jackson.

But Bankhead was also notorious for gang and crime activity, ranked by the website United Gangs as one of the "nine most dangerous housing projects in Atlanta." By the time it was demolished in the early '10s, Montero had already moved out. He later felt lucky to have left Bankhead when he did. "I didn't want to leave what I was used to, but it was better for me," Lil Nas X told Josh Eells at *Rolling Stone.* "If I would have stayed there, I would have fallen in with the wrong crowd." Still, Montero and his siblings didn't leave happily—his parents waged a custody battle, premised in part on his mother's drug abuse. Around age nine, Montero begrudgingly went to live with his father, a gospel singer, in the town of Austell in Cobb County, one of Atlanta's sprawling suburbs.

Young Montero eventually lost touch with his mother entirely. Years later, in an early Lil Nas X mixtape track called "Carry On," he addressed her deficient parenting: "How you leave your son all alone? See you every other month—can you hit a n***a phone? . . . You ain't even who you used to be, the person that I've known. Guess I have to carry on."

A self-described "class clown," Montero was a fairly diligent student through grade school. He started playing the trumpet in fourth grade and by junior high had made first chair. But he gave up the trumpet by the time he entered high school, because he "didn't want to look lame." Of course, by then Hill wasn't doing much outside class that didn't involve a screen. His father had by then moved the family to the town of Lithia Springs, about a half hour west of Atlanta, and it was there that Hill, when not attending Lithia Springs High School, became a devoted digital native and something of an internet savant.

Hill spent prodigious hours online—alone, but not alone—learning the folkways of 2010s social, viral, and especially meme culture. "I started to get into every side of the Internet around 13ish," Hill told NPR Music's Rodney Carmichael. "Not even intentionally, just learning how it works and how to use it to my advantage." Hill was fixated on finding his online persona, the alter ego that might bring him renown. This was "right around the time when memes started to become their own form of entertainment," he recalled. The goal was to tap into the kinds of Gen-Z-fluent microjokes (from Grumpy Cat to the Distracted Boyfriend) that would become infectious. "If you see something going around the Internet, people want to join in," he told *Time*'s Andrew Chow.

It was Nicki Minaj—the brassy rap queen with her army of celebrity-worshippers—who finally inspired Montero's first sticky online persona. Minaj's superfans or "stans," known as the Barbies or more commonly the Barbz, stood ready to defend Minaj from any perceived online slight. For more than two years, Hill ran a Barbz-affiliated Twitter account called @NasMaraj that trafficked in both Minaj-supporting content and straight-up viral memes engineered to generate community-reinforcing retweets by the thousands, a practice known as "tweetdecking." When Twitter, around 2018, started cracking down on accounts associated with tweetdecking, Hill switched one letter in his handle, launched a @NasMarai account, and kept on tweeting.

Eventually, @NasMaraj/@NasMarai morphed into Hill's Lil Nas X persona and served as an early platform for his home-grown musical experiments. In May 2018—while in his first and, it turned out, only year at the University of West Georgia—Hill uploaded his first Lil Nas X demo recording, "Shame," a standard-issue rap boast, to the music-sharing site SoundCloud. A couple of months later, it was followed by a full mixtape, the twenty-five-minute *Nasarati*. The EP already displayed Hill's culture-regurgitating wit: one track's beats were adapted from the coin-collecting sound in the video game *Sonic the Hedgehog*.

Like Twitter, SoundCloud was yet another digital playground for Montero: beyond its function as an audio app, SoundCloud drove a mid-'10s culture of melodic, emotional hip-hop commonly called "SoundCloud rap." The lyrics to Lil Nas X's aforementioned "Carry On" were quintessential SoundCloud rap—Hill angry at his mother but also nakedly wounded. The eighteen-year-old was savvy about his chosen medium. Hill used his Twitter profile, with its estimated six-figure follower count, to flog his mixtape tracks, sometimes even "sock-puppeting" to pretend he was promoting another person's music. He was impressed that a small online audience was already connecting with the tracks. "People were actually fucking with it," Hill told *Rolling Stone*.

The early results were enough to inspire Hill to drop out of college, which was boring him. When he told his father and stepmother in August 2018, just days before the fall semester of what would have been his sophomore year, that he'd already informed the University of West Georgia he wouldn't be coming back, their already testy relationship deteriorated. "My dad initially was like, 'There's a million rappers in this industry,'" Hill told *Time*. "They wanted me to go back to school." Instead, Montero left his father's house to go sleep on his sister's couch, living off a dwindling bank balance from a pair of summer jobs. The music wasn't generating enough traffic to get Hill paid. He grumbled that he could get more attention for a tweet than for a song.

It wasn't until October that Hill threw together the mixtape track that would change his life. Like virtually everything he did online, it was built for meme-ability. It was snarky but also sincere, wide-eyed, and charming, deliberately hokey but rather sweet. And it all came to him because he stumbled across a beat built out of a banjo sample.

Dutch teenager Kiowa Roukema—born in Purmerend, North Holland, the same year Montero Hill was born in Atlanta—posted beats online under the name YoungKio. Like many self-starting beatmakers, Roukema worked with FL Studio, successor to Fruity-Loops, a DIY music sequencer. Since its launch in 1997, Fruity-Loops/FL Studio, with its accessible visual interface, had raised at least two generations of self-taught producers in the rudiments of digital music creation, and for digerati like YoungKio, the learning curve was speedy. "In the beginning, I was trying to remake song instrumentals, just to learn and understand what they were doing," Roukema later told *Billboard*. "That made me learn really fast." Having taught himself how to create basic melodies, Young-Kio started playing with samples—the building blocks of American rap. "Hip-hop isn't really as big in the Netherlands as it is in the USA," he said. "So I just started putting my beats online to get an American following." That's when he stumbled on a recording that was conceived by its creator, from the jump, as a blank slate.

A decade earlier, Trent Reznor, founder and primary performer of platinum-selling industrial rock group Nine Inch Nails, had self-released an experimental album called *Ghosts I–IV*. The 2008 collection comprised four volumes of nondescript instrumental tracks, issued under a Creative Commons license. Reznor was inviting others to sample and build on the tracks. Each of the thirty-six tracks had a deliberately generic title denoting only the track number and volume in the set ("01 Ghosts I," "02 Ghosts I," continuing through "10 Ghosts II," and so forth). One of the last tracks, titled "34 Ghosts IV"—the album's longest, at just shy of six minutes—contained several segments, like classical movements. The most distinctive section was the sound of a plaintive banjo, plucked so delicately it resembled a Japanese kyoto.

YoungKio appreciated the melody's delicacy but proceeded with caution. "Normally, when I sample something I chop it, filter it—I turn it into something different," he told *Billboard*. "But this sample, I thought if I chopped this and filtered it, it's going to ruin it. I tried to keep as much of the originality of the sample, but I also wanted to have the trap vibe, so I sped it up. I didn't really have any country thoughts about it."

But Montero Hill definitely had "country thoughts." When he stumbled on YoungKio's beat on the audio marketplace Beat-Stars, the banjo—which had been made sprightlier by the Dutch producer and paired with a bassy thump—sounded like cowboy music. In other words, to the budding Lil Nas X, it sounded like a meme waiting to happen.

Nas named his creation "Old Town Road" because, he later told the *New York Times*, that name just sounded like a "real country place." He half-agrees with those who later dismissed the song as a novelty. From the jump, he saw the comic potential in juxta-posing a loping rap beat with cowpoke imagery. "Because it's two polar opposites coming together, it's funny no matter what it is," he later told *Time*. On the other hand, the lyric that Hill ultimately paired with the beat was coming from a sincere place, inside the heart and mind of a nineteen-year-old crashing on his sister's couch while pursuing a possibly crazy dream.

"I was picturing, like, a loner cowboy runaway," he told *Rolling Stone*. "Basically what I was going through, but in another lens." In a *Time* interview, Hill expanded on his inspiration, saying he wrote the song because he was "feeling like I was out of options. I was living with my sister. She was pretty much fed up with me being there. That's where the chorus lyric"—"I'm gonna ride 'til I can't no more"—"came from. It was me saying, 'I want to leave everything behind.' [Eventually] the 'Old Town Road' would be the symbol for success. The 'horse' would be, not having too much, but having what you have, in order to get to where you're trying to go. The 'can't nobody tell me nothing' part is referring to my parents: wanting me to go back to school, not thinking it's that likely for [me] to make it."

In late October 2019, Hill purchased YoungKio's beat for thirty dollars from BeatStars and took it to a tiny Atlanta studio, CinCoYo, that had a twenty-dollar-per-hour special on Tuesdays. (Hill told one reporter it was around Halloween, which would make the studio date Tuesday, October 30, 2018.) In that single one-hour session, Hill laid down his vocals in a knowingly exaggerated drawl, much twangier than his own Atlanta-born voice. He engineered the track, top to bottom, for virality. "It was the first song I genuinely formulated," he told *Rolling Stone*. "I was like, 'I gotta make it short, I gotta make it catchy, I gotta have quotable lines that people want to use as captions.' Especially with the 'horses in the back' line, I was like, 'This is something people are gonna say every day.'"

Montero Lamar Hill had organically created a proudly artificial cultural product: a heartfelt joke song, built out of a sample of an alternative rock band, sped up by a Dutch beatmaker Hill had never met, that Hill transformed into a country anthem with a hip-hop beat. Months later, in a *New Yorker* article titled "Lil Nas

X Is the Sound of the Internet, Somehow," critic Amanda Petrusich astutely noted:

> The entire philosophy of the Internet seems to be contained in the purposeful way that Nas X raps the phrase "I got the horses in the back," at the very start of "Old Town Road." He knows that it's a weird and funny and possibly absurd thing to say, and his voice is so flat and full of self-awareness that the line itself almost curls into a smirk—yet it is delivered earnestly!...This gets at something about the modern condition—that we have arrived at a moment in which self-definition trumps any other kind of categorization.

Less than six months later—on April 8, 2019, the day before Hill's twentieth birthday—*Billboard* would announce that "Old Town Road" was the No. 1 song in America. But the path Lil Nas X took to reach that milestone had curves and twists that none of his formulations could have accounted for. Hip-hop culture, internet culture, remix culture—all would play a role. But the cultural center Nas surely never thought he'd have to tangle with was based 250 miles northwest, in Nashville, Tennessee.

▶02 HIED 'til I Can't No More

A Brief History of Country and Race

IN 1962, RAY CHARLES RELEASED *Modern Sounds in Country and Western Music*, an album the music legend dreamed up to prove country and soul were "the same goddamn thing, exactly." As Charles saw it, whether played at a honky-tonk or at a dance hall on the chitlin' circuit, the cultures were aligned at the root. "Big hall, somebody be frying some chicken over in the corner, some fish maybe," he recalled to music historian Peter Guralnick. "You take country music, you take black music—[it's] the same thing, man."

Even at the time, *Modern Sounds* was regarded as a cross-cultural watershed. Trade magazines all concurred that the album was helping to popularize not only country crossover but country music itself. *Broadcasting* credited *Modern Sounds* with propelling "the Nashville Sound[, which] is sweeping the charts in national music popularity." *Variety* quoted legendary Nashville producer Owen Bradley, crediting country's improved sales in the early '60s to "barriers . . . broken by individuals like Ray Charles." Just weeks after its release, a Philadelphia record distributor told *Billboard* that *Modern Sounds* was "the hottest LP he's handled in years."

Billboard still charted monophonic and stereophonic albums on separate charts in 1962, and *Modern Sounds* topped both—the mono chart for a stunning fourteen weeks, the stereo chart for just one week but interrupting the yearlong run of the top-selling *West Side Story* film soundtrack. Charles's label, ABC Records, was persuaded to issue singles from the hard-to-categorize LP. They started with Charles's take on Nashville legend Don Gibson's 1958 country hit "I Can't Stop Loving You," and it was a smash. Charles's "Stop" topped the Hot 100 for five weeks and the R&B chart for ten. He went on to score with his sophisticated takes on "You Don't Know Me" (No. 2 pop, No. 5 R&B), "Born to Lose" (No. 41 pop), and "Careless Love" (No. 60 pop). Later that same year, Charles rush-released a second volume of *Modern Sounds* and scored again with his versions of the '30s country standard "You Are My Sunshine" (No. 7 pop, No. 1 R&B) and the Hank Williams classic "Your Cheating Heart" (No. 29 pop, No. 23 R&B).

Note that, among the *Billboard* pop and R&B chart statistics, I offer no Country chart peaks. There weren't any. The singles from *Modern Sounds in Country and Western Music* didn't chart country at all—not even "I Can't Stop Loving You," which had been a Top 10

Country hit for Gibson just four years earlier. As with Lil Nas X in 2019, it was taken as a given in Nashville in 1962 that Ray Charles did not belong in the Country format. Charles would not touch *Billboard*'s Country chart until the 1980s; when he finally did, it was mainly in duets with George Jones and Willie Nelson.

....

"Authenticity" is an ever-present, unavoidable theme across country music history. In a podcast episode about the cultural roots of country music, *Into the Zone* host Hari Kunzru notes: "I'm always on the alert when I hear the word *authentic*. It's a gatekeeping word—a word used to exclude. It's also racially loaded."

The goalposts of what qualifies as authentic country have shifted continually in the century since "hillbilly music" was coined as a distinct genre. "Country music is full of songs about little old log cabins that people have never lived in, the old country church that people have never attended," historian Bill C. Malone said in *Country Music*, the 2019 Ken Burns documentary miniseries. "Country music's staple, above all, is nostalgia—just a harkening back to the older way of life, either real or imagined." That wistfully imagined past, peddled as far back as the nineteenth century by white minstrel performers, included such Lost Cause totems as "darkies praising their masters" or "old Uncle Tom who wishes he was back in the old South."

Nonetheless, the roots of the music are deeply entwined with African American, even African, heritage. The banjo, essentially a drumhead plus strings, was originally fashioned from a gourd with a fretless neck and was brought to the States by slaves. "It's America," singer Rhiannon Giddens told documentarian Ken Burns, holding up a banjo, "but it's got Africa in it."

This heritage extends to the genre's formative singers and songs. The first major Grand Ole Opry star was multi-instrumentalist DeFord Bailey, the Opry's "Harmonica Wizard," whom the *Encyclopedia of Country Music* calls "the most significant Black country star before World War II." Or consider white country forefather and "singing brakeman" Jimmie Rodgers, who worked as a water boy for mostly Black railroad crews. Rodgers developed his seminal "blue yodel" by adopting the Alpine vocal sound as reimagined by Black (and blackface) singers.

A. P. Carter, patriarch of the foundational Carter Family, sourced much of the white trio's material in the late '20s by traveling through the South accompanied by a Black slide guitarist named Lesley Riddle, who referred to himself as Carter's "tape recorder." Riddle also taught sisters Sara and Maybelle Carter blues guitar stylings, as well as hymns that originated in Black Baptist and Pentecostal churches. "Will the Circle Be Unbroken," popularized by the Carter Family and one of country's most enduring songs, was formulated by A. P. Carter out of an old gospel tune that an African American minister had already reworked and recorded.

Bluegrass instigator Bill Monroe was mentored by guitarist, fiddler, and coal miner Arnold Schultz, an exceptional Black player who was welcomed by both white and Black audiences across Ohio County, Kentucky. At age twelve, Monroe followed Shultz to country dances, picking up techniques like unusual chord transitions and blues playing. Arnold Schultz died young, at forty-five, in 1931. Though it was Monroe who, roughly a dozen years later, coined and codified bluegrass, the International Bluegrass Music Association credits Schultz as a "godfather of bluegrass, a musical style he never heard."

Like Bill Monroe, country legend Hank Williams learned the rudiments of his instrument as a boy trailing after a seasoned Black performer: Montgomery street musician Rufus "Tee-Tot" Payne, who let the eight-year-old Williams follow his band as they roamed the streets playing for handouts. "All the music training I ever had was from him," Williams later said. After he moved to Nashville, Williams scored his first major hit with "Move It on Over" (No. 4 country, 1947), a song influenced by Tee-Tot that was later called a precursor to rock and roll.

"The Black musical influence in country music is immeasurable, as far as I'm concerned," the '80s–'90s country star Marty Stuart told Ken Burns. "If you took Mr. Lesley Riddle out of the A. P. Carter equation as a song-catcher and a song-gatherer; if you took Arnold Schultz out of Bill Monroe's life; or if you took Tee-Tot out of Hank Williams's life—just those three *alone*, look how different it would have turned out."

If Black performers were at the root of what made country actually authentic, many of the genre's seemingly traditional trap-

pings were more artificial—arrived at by happenstance, calcula-
tion, and belated adoption. The genre's cowboy iconography was
codified by Gene Autry, the "Singing Cowboy," who concocted his
persona in the '30s after trying his hand as a telegraph operator
and New York radio personality. Though he was mentored by self-
starting cowboy Will Rogers, Autry's persona truly went nationwide when he starred in a Hollywood-invented *Singing Cowboy*
film series. (The franchise spawned spinoff movie characters,
like singing cowgirl Dorothy Page, Mexican singing cowboy Tito
Guizar, and Black singing cowboy Herb Jeffries.)

Pedal steel, the archetypal instrument of country in the last half
of the twentieth century, was neither native to the genre nor play-
able without electrification. Its roots were in Hawaiian music, via
its predecessor the lap steel. "You can't play the pedal steel on a
farm," cultural critic Shuja Haider, writer of *The Believer*'s "The
Invention of Twang," told podcaster Hari Kunzru. "It's really kind
of a space-age sound—it sounds something like the theremin, or
even like a synthesizer."

Even the Nudie suit—the flamboyant, flame-bedecked outfits midcentury country stars would pair with boots and a cowboy hat—was a Ukrainian tailor's vision of American excess. The
Nudie was designed by Hollywood-based tailor Nutya Kotly-
renko, aka Nudie Cohn, originally from Kiev, and made famous
in the '50s by diminutive novelty singer Little Jimmy Dickens.

Black roots, faux-cowboy iconography, space-age instruments,
outlandish outfits: in 2019, a teenage Montero Lamar Hill would

try his hand at all of it. If anything, with his adoption of these tropes on "Old Town Road," Nas was being truer to the music's history than many mainstream twenty-first-century country stars, who typically prefer ballcaps to cowboy hats and employ funk bass, synthesizers, and electronic production more overtly than the mild hip-hop beats undergirding "Old Town Road." A study of country music instrumentation by streaming-music service Pandora—using data from its musical genome project, and released in 2018, the year before "Road" exploded on the charts— found country hits with a "funk influence" began increasing in frequency starting in the '70s (examples included Willie Nelson's "Shotgun Willie" and Dolly Parton's "Gettin' Happy"), and those with synthesizers exploded in the early 2010s (e.g., Keith Urban's "Little Bit of Everything").

Ironically, attempts by Black artists to cross over in country typically adhere more closely to traditionalism than those of current country hitmakers. When Ray Charles made his foray into *Country and Western* he was following nearly a decade of growth in the so-called Nashville sound. Pioneered by producers Owen Bradley and Chet Atkins, the Nashville sound featured soft piano, glistening strings, and plush background vocals by the likes of the Anita Kerr Singers or the Jordanaires. Though Charles recorded in New York and Los Angeles, his arrangements were directly modeled after the Nashville sound, and his team sourced repertoire, like Don Gibson's "I Can't Stop Loving You," from a range of Nashville publishers. What made the album distinctive was Charles's bluesy vocal phrasing, which one can liken to Lil Nas X's rap beats—the one element added to what is otherwise a fairly traditional country recording. It is this element that allows authenticity gatekeepers to claim the result isn't (ain't) country.

In her essay "Making Country Modern" from *Hidden in the Mix: The African American Presence in Country Music*, Diane Pecknold draws a distinction between the country music industry—which long sought to promote "mainstream respectability . . . a progressive, modern position on race"—and its radio programmers. When the Country Music Association was founded in 1958, its primary goal was elevating class perceptions of the music's audience. "The CMA sought to counter the prevailing stereotype that country listeners were ignorant, barefoot hillbillies," Pecknold writes, "whether they still lived in rural areas or had migrated to the city." Accordingly, the CMA embraced Charles's *Modern Sounds* as evidence of the growing sophistication of country as a genre.

It was at the radio disc jockey level—closer to the ground, so to speak, to the extent that DJs reflected listener preference—that Ray Charles hit a wall. By the end of 1962, even as the trades were hailing *Modern Sounds* as one of the year's top musical events, their polls of country DJs found them ignoring Charles's material entirely, failing to list it among their top picks for the year. To be fair, the album's hybridized material had initially confused R&B disc jockeys as well—Charles later claimed Black DJs had resisted the material until "I Can't Stop Loving You" became too big to ignore. Charles's track record at the format meant Black radio DJs came around. Country jockeys had no such incentive to play material from a format visitor, even when he had the top album in America for months.

In the years between Ray Charles and Lil Nas X, performers of color were embraced in the country format only when they played the Nashville game by Nashville rules—and then, only sparingly. In the wake of Charles's blockbuster sales, a wave of '60s Black stars tried country material or recorded in Nashville, including Solomon Burke, Esther Phillips, Carla Thomas, and Sam Cooke. None of this material made the Country charts, either, although this movement did eventually foster the development of what Charles Hughes, in his book *Country Soul: Making Music and Making Race in the American South*, terms the "country-soul triangle" of recording centers in Nashville, Memphis, and Muscle Shoals, Alabama.

Then there was Charley Pride—easily the top Black performer in country history (29 No. 1 hits, a dozen gold albums). When Pride broke in the '60s, it took careful strategy and pressure tactics by white gatekeepers to get him over at radio. Chet Atkins signed Pride to RCA Records, which issued his early singles with no photos or any word of Pride's race. It helped that, as Hughes notes, Pride had a "classic honky-tonk sound"; Atkins reinforced the image by billing the Mississippian's first records under "Country Charley Pride." Format stalwart Faron Young (who, according to Ken Burns's *Country Music*, complimented Pride the day he met him by marveling, "Here I am, singin' with a jig, and I don't mind") went further, challenging a station manager to take his own records off if they wouldn't play Pride's. The singer's audience-mollifying charm also didn't hurt—Pride greeted the crowd at one concert with this intro: "Ladies and gentlemen, I realize it's kinda unique, me coming out here on a country music show wearing this permanent tan."

Other than Pride, country produced no major Black stars in the closing decades of the twentieth century. Ray Charles returned to the format in the '80s, long after his pop and R&B hitmaking days waned, as a fifty-something artist. A duet with Clint Eastwood from the latter's 1980 film *Any Which Way You Can* got Charles on the Country chart for the first time ever. Five years later a pairing with Willie Nelson on "Seven Spanish Angels" finally gave Charles a No. 1 country hit.

It took until 2008 for a third Black performer to reach No. 1 on *Billboard*'s Hot Country Songs, when former Hootie and the Blowfish frontman Darius Rucker reached the top of the chart with his debut country single, "Don't Think I Don't Think about It." This was far from Rucker's recording debut; with the Blowfish, he'd recorded one of the biggest pop albums of all time, 1994's bar-rock, country-friendly *Cracked Rear View*. (While Hootie was on a brief hiatus in the early '00s, Rucker had tried recording an R&B album, which flopped.) Even more than Ray Charles or Charley Pride, Rucker played the Nashville game straight down the middle, cowriting virtually all of his country debut's tracks with established songwriters like Chris DuBois, Clay Mills, and a young Chris Stapleton. The result: the first country No. 1 by a Black artist since Charles's Willie Nelson duet in 1985, and the first *solo* Black chart-topper in a quarter century, dating to Pride's twenty-ninth and final No. 1, 1983's "Night Games."

As Rucker has scored seven more country No. 1s over the last dozen years, including the 2013 country-rock crossover smash "Wagon Wheel," his Nashville-dutiful template has opened a lane for other Black artists, including late-'10s Country chart-toppers Kane Brown, Jimmie Allen, and Blanco Brown. What distinguishes these artists' hits (e.g., Kane Brown's "What Ifs" and "Good as You"; Allen's "Best Shot" and "Make Me Want To"; Blanco Brown's "The Git Up") from Lil Nas X's "Old Town Road" is only the lack of a synthesized trap beat. All of these Black acts have topped the Country charts by eschewing or sublimating any modern pop, R&B, or hip-hop influences in a quest for the terrestrial-radio acceptance that still drives country fandom.

Which is not to say country radio is completely free of hip-hop. It's just that Black artists, by and large, aren't the ones getting rap played on those airwaves. *White* country stars are—which prompts a whole separate chapter in the story that spawned Lil Nas X.

▶ 03 FLY 'til I Can't No More

The Collision and Cross-Pollination
of Rap and Country

IN 2001, WARREN MATHIS, a white man from LaGrange, Georgia, released his debut album, *Dark Days, Bright Nights*, under the name Bubba Sparxxx. AllMusic would call him "the redneck version of Eminem." Sparxxx mixed "hick-hop" lyrics ("The South has always been Dirty—but now it's gettin' ugly") with thumping beats supplied by a Black production team that included Timothy "Timbaland" Mosley, famed for his work with Missy Elliott and Aaliyah; and Organized Noize, the Atlanta-based team affiliated with OutKast. The video for Sparxxx's lead single, the Timbaland-produced "Ugly," featured Bubba and his crew, white and Black, splashing around in a muddy pigpen with actual pigs. "Ugly" charted well at Top 40 and rap radio. It didn't chart Country at all.

Seven years later, a producer who'd worked on Sparxxx's debut—Shannon Houchins, a white man who called himself Fat Shan—produced the debut album from another white rapper, Colt Ford from Athens, Georgia. Fat Shan paired Ford with established country singers to court Nashville credibility. The standout track on Ford's 2008 debut was "Dirt Road Anthem," a honky-tonk rap in which Ford dropped hick-hop bars at triple-time speed ("Sit back and think about them good ole days / The way we were raised and our southern ways"), and the chorus, sung by Brantley Gilbert, was sweet, melodic, and squarely suited for country radio. Only the limited resources of Ford's independent label could explain why the catchy "Dirt Road Anthem" wasn't a hit in '08.

Two more years after that, "Dirt Road Anthem" was rerecorded twice: first by Gilbert, the original hook-singer, this time with Ford listed as the featured act. Gilbert's version didn't chart, either, but it offered a template for how the song could retain Ford's rap while going fully country. The second 2010 cover was by established Nashville star Jason Aldean, who vocalized the whole song himself—singing the chorus *and* rapping the verses. Aldean's "Dirt Road Anthem," issued as the third single from his *My Kinda Party* album, topped *Billboard*'s Hot Country Songs in July 2011.

The path from Bubba Sparxxx to Jason Aldean exemplifies how a certain kind of rap became acceptable in country music. The further hick-hop veered away from actual rap production—and Black cocreators—the easier it registered on Country radio. In essence, a decade later, Lil Nas X would condense this racial-identity tussle into a single song.

....

The charge commonly laid on "Old Town Road" by Nashville partisans is that it was comical, a novelty, and hence disrespectful to country tradition. The truth was, Lil Nas X was channeling a decades-long history of cross-pollination between hip-hop and country—one that started decades before his birth and was always equal parts comedy and comity.

The integration of cowboy iconography and Black music during the funk and early hip-hop eras was largely cosmetic at first. *Black Country Music* author Francesca Royster recalls, "Funksters mixed cowboy style into their looks during the eighties: Rick James and Con Funk Shun; Earth, Wind and Fire; and the Commodores— all rocking fringe and sometimes cowboy hats on *Don Kirshner's Rock Concert* or MTV . . . Cameo's 'She's Strange' takes place in an abandoned Old West saloon. This style was a Black cowboy style without really needing the cowboys." Boston electro-funksters the Jonzun Crew took the iconography a bit further on their 1983 hit "Space Cowboy" (No. 12 R&B), which—though it was sung through and not rapped—foreshadowed later hybridizations by mixing hip-hop–style breakbeats with a tall tale of an "outer-space outlaw . . . with a laser gun."

The earliest undisputed popular mashup of rap with cowboy culture came in 1984 with "Rappin' Duke," a novelty single by

Shawn Brown, a Chicago-born, LA-based comedian. Brown did an intentionally wooden John Wayne impression, and the song's refrain—"duh-HA, duh-HAA," parodying Wayne's stiff movie laughter—complemented the song's simple 808 beat. The video portrayed a cowpoke roaming the range with a boombox. Brown's bars were rife with Saturday-matinee western tropes: "Sure, I rustled some cattle and tended the sheep / But my main concern was rappin' to the beat." The single scored decent airplay for a novelty record, hitting No. 73 on *Billboard*'s R&B chart in the spring of 1985 (an '86 follow-up, "Duke Is Back," charted too, a bit higher). Seemingly destined to be a rap-lore footnote, "Rappin' Duke" holds a special place in the heart of hip-hop fans, thanks to the late rapper Christopher Wallace, aka Biggie Smalls or the Notorious B.I.G. In the first verse of "Juicy," Biggie's wistful 1994 breakthrough hit, he reminisces: "Remember 'Rappin' Duke'? 'Duh-ha, duh-ha' / You never thought that hip-hop would take it this far."

In the decade-plus after "Rappin' Duke," rap's country invocations were still centered around hokey cowboy imagery. Sir Mix-a-Lot's 1986 twelve-inch single "Square Dance Rap"—issued a half dozen years before his smash "Baby Got Back"—attempted a version of southern line-dance calling but undercut its authenticity with sped-up Chipmunk-style vocals (never mind that Mix-a-Lot was from Seattle). Kool Moe Dee's hit "Wild, Wild West" (No. 4 R&B, 1988), despite a video replete with cowboy imagery, was mostly a straight-up New York street-rap record; its tales of gunplay were really about showdowns on the West Side of Manhattan. A little over a decade later, Will Smith's own "Wild, Wild West," a glossy pop-rap chart-topper from the flop film of the same name, featured Kool Moe Dee reprising his 1988 hook; the track was mostly built from a sample of Stevie Wonder's '70s soul-funk classic "I Wish." For most of the '90s gangsta-rap era, the Old West trope proved durable—Intelligent Hoodlum's "Posse (Shoot 'em Up)" in 1993, Mo Thugs Family's "Ghetto Cowboy" featuring Bone Thugs-n-Harmony in 1998—but these hits largely resembled traditional urban boom-bap and were essentially twang-free.

At the turn of the millennium, what drew rap closer to country were a pair of cultural pivots: rap's center of gravity moved south, and hip-hop welcomed white performers with a country lean.

In the latter category, Robert Ritchie, aka Kid Rock, is a key liminal figure given his promiscuous genre-hopping. Starting as a straight-up rapper in 1990, it took Kid Rock four albums and a couple of format tweaks before he issued his 1998 diamond-certified blockbuster *Devil without a Cause*, which made him both thrashier and twangier at the same time. Each single was a little more country-indebted than the last. After the shrieking "Bawitdaba" got the Kid on rock radio and MTV, 1999's "Cowboy" was a rap-rock-country mashup with not only Wild West lyrics but also some actual pickin'-and-grinnin' on banjo and slide guitar. And his 2000 hit "Only God Knows Why"—the album's biggest chart hit (No. 19 Hot 100, No. 5 Mainstream Rock)—was a full-on country-rock ballad with robotic Auto-tuned vocals; it featured no rapping. In other words, Kid Rock was pulling away from rap before the promotional cycle for his breakthrough album was even over. By the time of Rock's 2002 album *Cocky* and its smash ballad "Picture," a duet with country singer Allison Moorer (a pop version featured Sheryl Crow), he'd shifted toward mid-tempo country-pop and the right-wing-leaning barroom rock he is now known for. "Cowboy" in '99 was the closest he came to letting straight-up rap and southern-fried twang coexist on a hit.

The more pivotal shift was in hip-hop itself. Southern rap's shot heard 'round the world came at the 1995 Source Awards. As Atlanta's OutKast accepted a Best New Group trophy—amid heavy boos from the New York crowd—the duo's André Benjamin (the future André 3000) closed his acceptance speech by declaring, "The South got somethin' to say." This turned out to be perhaps the most prescient statement in hip-hop history, as rap's locus shifted inexorably from the East and West Coasts to the South, with Atlanta as its capital (the same city Montero Hill was born into in 1999). On OutKast's seminal hit "Rosa Parks" (No. 55 Hot 100, No. 19 R&B, 1999), André and partner Antwan "Big Boi" Patton were rapping over porch-stomp percussion and country-blues guitar, with a full-on hoedown at the bridge featuring harmonica by Reverend Robert Hodo, André's stepfather.

"Rosa Parks" had the most overt pure-country instrumentation on a rap single to date, but it wasn't the last. Nappy Roots, a sextet formed in Louisville in the mid-'90s when the members were attending Western Kentucky University, hit paydirt in 2002

with their platinum major-label debut *Watermelon, Chicken &*
Gritz. Its lead single, "Po' Folks" (No. 21 pop, No. 13 R&B), featuring soulful vocals from Charlotte R&B singer Anthony Hamilton, paired a gentle, country-lite guitar strum with heartfelt lyrics about rural poverty: "Sometimes I ask myself, was I made for
the world? . . . Front porch, chillin' broke, country folk—I'm Nappy
with my ways, yo."

Southern rap producers and MCs were threading a fine needle.
The country audience's melodic requirements were more than
a flossy, thumping rap joint could bear. Post-OutKast, "southern
rap" typically meant skittering proto-trap beats from the likes of
Master P's No Limit empire in New Orleans, or Atlanta microphone
fiends like Ludacris. Luda would nod to his heritage with farm
sounds like a crowing rooster on "Saturday (Ooooh! Ooooh!)," but
the rest of the track had to boom like a strip club. This dilemma
between hip-hop and country credibility ultimately limited the
trajectory of the aforementioned Bubba Sparxxx, who tried to
center both genres in his music. Nothing he recorded with country arrangements boosted his career—Sparxxx's 2003 album
Deliverance only went deeper into country, such as the banjo-
and-fiddle-led "Comin' Round," an interpolation of "To See You
Coming 'Round the Bend" by the Yonder Mountain String Band.
Deliverance was off the charts in just over two months. Three
years later, what finally broke Sparxxx on the radio was a catchy
but doctrinaire Dirty South jam, "Ms. New Booty" (No. 7 pop and
R&B, 2006). Sporting a guest refrain from Atlanta crunk kings the

Ying Yang Twins, "Booty" had scarcely any country in it. Sparxxx was now attesting to his urban cred: "Yeah, I'm a country boy, but that big-city bottom fill me up with joy."

The hick-hop hybrid wasn't much more successful in the other direction: incubating a rapper from within the belly of Nashville. The country-rap hype of 2005 was Cowboy Troy—an affiliate of the quirky mid-'00s country collective Muzik Mafia, led by iconoclastic hitmaking duo Big & Rich, famed for the cheeky "Save a Horse (Ride a Cowboy)." Born Troy Lee Coleman III, the towering Texan took the stage in full cowboy drag—hat, denim, gingham shirt—rapping in a friendly drawl over country-rock arrangements like a Black George Strait with flow. His *Loco Motive* album, thanks to its Muzik Mafia bona fides, debuted at No. 2 on Country Albums and rode the chart for the better part of a year, but unlike Sparxxx, Troy never achieved a gold album. Perhaps Troy's most impressive achievement was getting on country radio: "I Play Chicken with the Train" hit No. 48 on Hot Country Songs. Its meager four-week run was the most rapping Country radio audiences would hear until Jason Aldean covered "Dirt Road Anthem" a half decade later.

Even if country and rap couldn't crossbreed their way onto Country radio, the two genres kept colliding in the '00s and '10s. St. Louis rapper Nelly's acclaimed 2004 smash "Over and Over" featured soulful, high-lonesome vocals from Nashville megastar Tim McGraw. It reached No. 3 on the Hot 100 and topped playlists at both Top 40 and rhythmic pop stations, but it wasn't promoted to Country stations. A decade later, Nelly returned the favor to Nashville, recording a remix of bro-country duo Florida Georgia Line's smash single "Cruise." The duo's original was a No. 1 Country hit in 2012, but as with "Over and Over," this Nelly remix was only promoted to Top 40 radio; it gave Florida Georgia Line a Top Five pop hit in 2013. Irrepressible striver Colt Ford kept trying to evolve from hick-hop novelty to legitimate hitmaker, rapping alongside everyone from country mainstays Jake Owen and Jason Aldean to his white country-rap forebear Bubba Sparxxx. A 2013 Bubba–Colt posse cut, "Country Folks," laid bare the commonality they saw in rap and country audiences: "Been doing this for some years, y'all so late / Bangin' OutKast and a little George Strait." At the peak of bro-country, programmers lightly spun Ford's twangy bangers as a diversion, but his tracks never took center stage. (The less said about Brad Paisley's well-meant, ill-conceived "Accidental Racist" with rap legend LL Cool J—a 2013 single that was chum for social media longer than its brief two-week Country chart run—the better.)

Underlying this checkered track record for country-rap crossover were questions of genre and race. Even when whites were doing the rapping, country radio programmers were engaging in gatekeeping and authenticity-policing, playing hick-hop only selectively. Such intersectional concerns lurked below the surface for most of the 2010s, until Black artists began forcing the issue by invoking country tropes toward the end of the decade, even more overtly than OutKast or Nappy Roots did at the turn of the millennium. This was the last piece of the puzzle for Lil Nas X and "Old Town Road."

Leading the charge in the mid-'10s was Atlanta's Young Thug (born Jeffery Lamar Williams), whom Nas would later credit as the forefather of the "country-trap" sound. An eccentric rapper with a unique vocal tone, Thug widened the lane for the cross-pollination of country tropes into rap jams. On his acclaimed 2017 mixtape *Beautiful Thugger Girls*, which Thug regarded as a "singing album," the leadoff track, "Family Don't Matter," opens with an exuberant "Yee-haw!" and only gets twangier from there. Other 2017–18 country-trap tracks contemporaneous with, or inspired by, Young Thug came from SoundCloud rappers Mir Fontane, with the trippily twangy "Down by the River"; Lil Tracy, with his laconic, backwoodsy "Like a Farmer"; and Mysticphonk, with the rustic "haunt u," a trap-rock jam with keening guitars and a canyon-deep Lil Peep vocal.

Among this wave of viral rap hits, "Like a Farmer" was perhaps the most obvious antecedent to "Old Town Road," not only in its twang but also in its sense of humor and even its lyrical hook: "I got horses in my car, just like a farmer . . . I got some horses in this truck, keep up." The echoes in Nas's "I got the horses in the back" are hard to miss. In a video interview with the lyrics transcription and interpretation website Genius, Lil Tracy (born Jazz Butler) admitted, "I don't think I really had a point—I was just trolling, like it was a joke." A drunk Tracy and his friends were messing with "country-people impersonations" when he stumbled across a folksy beat, by a beatmaker calling himself Gren8. Tracy was inspired to freestyle a faux–Deep South accent over that beat. (Recall Nas stumbling across the oddly country-like Nine Inch Nails beat from Dutchman YoungKio and deciding to adopt a southern accent.)

Released in the spring of 2018, "Like a Farmer" racked up some 2 million SoundCloud streams in six months. A remix with Philadelphia rapper Lil Uzi Vert did even better, garnering another 7.6 million streams by the fall of 2018. That was the very moment Lil Nas X was recording his own comic tale of horses in the back, the song that would redefine country-trap as pure pop, resulting in the longest-dominating Hot 100 hit ever.

▶ **04** REIFIED 'til I Can't No More

What a No. 1 Hit Meant as the Hot 100 Evolved

IN 1995, SONY MUSIC WAS ON A ROLL, pulling off all-time records on *Billboard*'s charts that were previously thought impossible. In its thirty-seven-year history, the Hot 100 had never seen a single debut at No. 1. By the end of '95, Sony had created the conditions for three singles to enter on top.

That summer, Michael Jackson, signed to Sony's Epic Records, achieved a pair of record-high debuts, back to back: a No. 5 entry for his duet with sister Janet, "Scream"; and, more remarkably, a No. 1 debut for Jackson's ballad "You Are Not Alone." Prior to 1995, no single had ever debuted higher on the Hot 100 than the Beatles' "Let It Be," which entered the chart at No. 6 in 1970, a full quarter century earlier. The Beatles had achieved their feat in the analog era of the charts, when singles were on 45-RPM vinyl and retailers normally took weeks to report strong sales.

By the '90s, when *Billboard*'s charts were computerized, Sony used savvy chart gamesmanship to make Jackson's high debuts possible. The label promoted the songs to radio for nearly a month, without releasing the singles in record stores. Under *Billboard* rules at the time, singles could not appear on the Hot 100 until they hit retail. Having built up their airplay, Epic then dropped the singles in stores, knowing diehard Jackson fans would snap them up. It was now possible for a song with blockbuster sales to generate an instant high debut—even as high as No. 1.

This gambit worked so well that another Sony label, Columbia, pulled the same trick that fall with back-to-back singles by Mariah Carey. "Fantasy," an up-tempo pop song built out of a sample of the Tom Tom Club's "Genius of Love," and "One Sweet Day," a gospel-flavored, melisma-heavy ballad pairing Carey with then-hot vocal group Boyz II Men, both built up their airplay for weeks before arriving in record stores. Both entered the Hot 100 at No. 1. But while Jackson's "You Are Not Alone" had spent only a week on top, the Carey singles settled in for epic runs: eight weeks for "Fantasy," and an astounding sixteen weeks for "One Sweet Day." That run for "Day" was the longest any single had ever spent on top of the chart. It was as if Sony—through entirely legal means—had hacked the Hot 100.

The "One Sweet Day" record for No. 1 longevity, set in 1996, would hold for nearly a quarter century. In 2019, it was finally broken by Lil Nas X's "Old Town Road," which spent nineteen weeks on top. (Notably, "Road" was also issued by Sony's Columbia label.) Just as the game had evolved between the Beatles' day and Mariah Carey's, Montero Hill took advantage of a massive shift in chart rules, from physical to digital. He played the game better than anyone had before.

....

A bit of history: *The Billboard*, as the magazine was originally called, was founded in 1894 to track the amusements business—circuses, fairgrounds, vaudeville. By the Great Depression, the magazine had diversified into the fast-growing music business, including the song-sheet sales fueling Tin Pan Alley. *Billboard*'s first weekly "National List of Best Selling Retail Records" launched in July 1940. (The first-ever Billboard No. 1 song: bandleader Tommy Dorsey's "I'll Never Smile Again," with lead vocals by a young Frank Sinatra.) By the 1950s, the magazine ran separate charts to track best-selling records in stores, most-played songs by "[disc] jockeys," and most-played songs in jukeboxes.

On August 4, 1958, *Billboard* launched the Hot 100 as the "first true blend" of sales-plus-spins. (The first-ever Hot 100 No. 1: Ricky Nelson's "Poor Little Fool.") Ultimately, what made the Hot 100 authoritative—what made it catch on not just within the music industry but also with the general public—was the balance of its airplay-plus-sales system. The songs doing well at radio and retail are broadly similar at any given time, but different enough from each other that averaging them together gives a robust picture of the current state of the hit parade. Sales data capture what

I call **active fandom**—picture the most obsessive fan, the one guaranteed to buy a pop idol's latest single in its first week, from the Beatles in 1964 to Justin Bieber in 2010—while radio reflects **passive fandom**: the way songs float through the ether—a passing car, a local retailer, a beach boombox—and dominate our culture. (Lacking robust jukebox data, *Billboard* would drop the category by the end of the '50s.)

The Hot 100 helped entrench *Billboard* as the bible of the music business, a position it still holds. There was no lack of competition: *Billboard* outlasted industry magazines *Cash Box*, *Radio & Records*, and *Record World/Music Vendor*, each with its own charts, as well as numerous smaller tip sheets. The Hot 100's hegemony was also helped along by its adoption as the basis for the syndicated radio show *American Top 40*, hosted by legendary broadcaster Casey Kasem starting in 1970.

In the old days, the Hot 100 was both faster and slower. It was faster, because single releases turned over more frequently. A Top 10 or even No. 1 hit could rise, peak, and fall off the chart in a three-to-four-month cycle. For example, the Beatles' "Yesterday," a 1965 No. 1 hit, was on and off the Hot 100 in eleven weeks. That was typical for the time—No. 1s by such totemic acts as the Supremes ("I Hear a Symphony," ten weeks), the Rolling Stones ("Paint It Black," eleven weeks) and Simon & Garfunkel ("Mrs. Robinson," thirteen weeks) cycled swiftly through radio playlists and record-store sales reports.

Yet the Hot 100 was also slower, because songs took longer to climb the chart—usually at least a month or two. Debuts in the Top 10 were extraordinarily rare, No. 1 debuts basically impossible. The chart relied on a system of phoning (or, later, faxing) retailers and radio stations for sales reports and playlists, and it took a matter of weeks for these fallible humans to register that something was becoming a hit. Long stays at No. 1 were also rare. It took until 1977 for a single to spend as many as ten weeks on top: Debby Boone's mawkish megaballad "You Light Up My Life" was the first, and four years later, Olivia Newton-John repeated the feat with her aerobicized ten-week 1981 blockbuster "Physical."

In short, prior to the 1990s, hitmaking was understood to be a gradual-rise, quick-falloff game, and the public's song appetite was thought to be a new hit from a star roughly every quarter year. Then *Billboard* rebooted its charts around computerized, more precise song-and-spin tallies—and the industry realized a lot of those assumptions were wrong, maybe even backward.

In 1991, *Billboard* began licensing a data technology called SoundScan, a system built on Universal Product Code (UPC) scanners at record-store cash registers. The UPC barcode scanner, commonplace since the '80s in supermarkets, was still rolling out to music retail. At the start of the '90s, many record stores still relied on manual price-tag checkout. When *Billboard* converted its album chart to SoundScan data in the issue dated May 25, 1991, SoundScan's penetration of music retail had reached 85 percent; only the smallest retailers were allowed to continue submitting old-fashioned sales rankings to *Billboard*. (Then an independent company that licensed data to *Billboard*, SoundScan was eventually acquired by market-measurement giant Nielsen, which was itself acquired in the late '90s by the same parent company as *Billboard*. After a long period as Nielsen SoundScan, the music-tallying system is now branded by *Billboard* sister company Luminate.)

Despite some carping from the industry over this shift, even without full market penetration, the data from SoundScan crushed the old manual-tabulation system for accuracy. The SoundScan album chart upended previously held beliefs about record promotion. Under the old chart system, hit albums would debut somewhere in the middle of the chart, then rise to an eventual peak; even No. 1 LPs by superstars took a few weeks to a couple of months to reach the top. SoundScan revealed that most hit albums open like hit movies: at the top. No. 1 album debuts went from rare to commonplace. Since 1991, most weeks on the Billboard 200 album chart, the No. 1 album debuted there; and the great majority of LPs open at their peak position.

Later in 1991, *Billboard* tackled the more involved task of converting the Hot 100 to SoundScan. Because the song chart factors in not just singles sales but also radio airplay, *Billboard* added to the mix a new radio-tallying technology called Broadcast Data Systems (BDS), which used an embryonic version of the "audio fingerprint" technology now commonplace in the smartphone app Shazam. In its accuracy, BDS did for radio what SoundScan did for retail. In essence, it eliminated the so-called paper add, wherein a radio station was incentivized (usually by a record label) to report a track to *Billboard* it wasn't actually playing much, or at all.

On the more data-rich Hot 100, the effects of the new Sound-Scan/BDS regime were as epochal as they were for the album chart—but also contradictory. On the one hand, songs could break faster. High debuts and big leaps up the chart, driven by computerized singles sales, were now possible. The old system relied on ranked reports without specific sales tallies—so the magnitude of a retail chain's top-selling single couldn't be reflected. Now SoundScan gave *Billboard* an exact count of just how many physical copies a song shifted; if a single went from 50,000 sold in a week to 150,000 the next, the chart would reflect it quickly. On the other hand, paradoxically, hit songs would linger much *longer* on the new Hot 100. Once radio picked up on a song, stations would continue rotating it far longer than station reports previously reflected.

In other words, the old gradual-rise, fast-drop pattern of the analog Hot 100 was now, essentially, reversed. Big hits would break quickly, then hang on to the chart for unprecedented stretches. This was likely the way hits had behaved all along, but the analog charts did not reflect that reality. Several all-time Hot 100 longevity benchmarks were reset quickly under the new methodology. Within the first eighteen months, the record for most weeks at No. 1 was broken twice: thirteen weeks for Boyz II Men's yearning R&B ballad "End of the Road" (1992), then fourteen weeks for Whitney Houston's titanic cover of Dolly Parton's "I Will Always Love You" (1992–93). The aforementioned records by Michael Jackson and Mariah Carey—the first-ever No. 1 debut with "You Are Not Alone," and the longest-ever No. 1 (sixteen weeks) with "One Sweet Day," respectively—would not have been possible without SoundScan.

But the Hot 100 did not remain static even after computerization. The chart underwent many more major rule changes, all of which had an impact on the chart patterns of early twenty-first-century hits. These changes would eventually all redound to the benefit of "Old Town Road."

The most significant change came with the advent of digital music. At the turn of the millennium, Napster popularized the idea of MP3 downloading—albeit in illicit, non-industry-sanctioned form. In 2003, Apple created a legitimate, monetized market for downloads with the launch of the iTunes Music Store. Within a year, thanks to the app's consumer-friendly ninety-nine-cent song price, dollar downloads were booming—so in early 2005, *Billboard* added digital sales to the Hot 100. This energized the chart considerably. Consumers' ability to satisfy song cravings instantly allowed songs to make even bigger leaps up the chart.

A half decade after that, when Spotify arrived in America, the streaming era on the charts began—and *Billboard* made an even more fundamental change to the chart's math. To recap, from its founding in 1958 to the last half of the '00s, the Hot 100 measured, broadly, just two things: radio airplay and retail singles. While *Billboard* had changed many elements of the underlying data—accounting for new radio formats and the transition from AM to FM, the advent of various physical single formats, the SoundScan-era computerization of sales-and-airplay tallying and, finally, the invention of the retail download store—in all that time, radio was still radio, and the fundamental act of paying a buck or two to own a copy of a song stayed the same.

Streaming added a new ingredient to the mix. What distinguishes streaming from all other forms of music discovery and consumption is its basic premise: user song *choice*, without song *ownership*. Indeed, what streaming most resembles is that old standby, the jukebox—instant gratification, no retention. From the dawn of the internet, futurists have hyped its potential as a "celestial jukebox." In the age of Spotify and YouTube, this mission was fulfilled.

So, more than fifty years after *Billboard* stopped tracking jukebox plays, jukebox-like consumption became the third ingredient in a formerly two-ingredient Hot 100 formula. In 2012, *Billboard* launched an On-Demand Songs chart that ranked song plays at services ranging from Spotify to such now-defunct services as Rhapsody and MOG. A year later, *Billboard* expanded the category with a more comprehensive Streaming Songs chart, to which it added music video plays on YouTube and Vevo. The 2013 methodology launched with a bang when it instantly generated a No. 1 hit, Baauer's "Harlem Shake," that was fueled by user-generated video and would never have made the Top 10, let alone No. 1, without video play. By the late '10s, as Spotify took over the music industry, streaming went from less than one-third of the data making up the Hot 100 to more than half, dwarfing radio and sales.

All these shifts in the cadence of hitmaking help explain how, in 2019, Mariah Carey and Boyz II Men's longevity record atop the Hot 100 was finally beaten by "Old Town Road." Every change to the Hot 100 formula over the prior three decades contributed to Lil Nas X's success: more accurate music-biz data, the snow-balling of that data to create faster chart breaks and longer chart runs, the invention of digital music and corresponding creation of the instant-gratification hit, and the addition of jukebox-like playability and video elements to the chart formula. Even accounting for the song's broad, cross-genre appeal, it is hard to imagine "Old Town Road" becoming a chart blockbuster without these prior chart evolutions.

But in early 2019, Lil Nas X's hit first generated headlines not due to its performance on the all-encompassing Hot 100 but due to its appearance—and disappearance—on *Billboard*'s genre-specific charts: R&B and especially Country. The rules for these charts turned out to be much more fraught.

►05 DIVIDE 'til I Can't No More

Genre Charts, Data, and Identity

IN 2014, *BILLBOARD*'S EDITORS made a categorical decision about Mark Ronson and Bruno Mars's hit "Uptown Funk!" They were not going to classify it as an R&B song or allow it to compete on their Hot R&B/Hip-Hop Songs chart, even though "Uptown Funk!" is an homage to turn-of-the-'80s R&B, from Rick James to Zapp to the Gap Band. It's so indebted to that sound, in fact, that the Gap Band's members made a legal claim against Ronson and Mars and settled for a cowriting credit.

In early 2015, as "Uptown Funk!" began a long run at No. 1 on the pop chart (fourteen weeks), it also began breaking at Black radio. Even in the face of this acceptance by the R&B audience, *Billboard* still would not allow "Uptown Funk!" onto Hot R&B/Hip-Hop Songs. Their director of charts said he considered the song "a pop hit that is crossing over to R&B radio."

By April 2015, "Uptown Funk!" ranked fifth at R&B/hip-hop radio stations, with a bigger Black radio audience than such major genre hits as Nicki Minaj's "Feeling Myself" and Drake's "How about Now." Yet Ronson and Mars's hit never appeared on *Billboard*'s flagship R&B chart. Had it been allowed onto Hot R&B/Hip-Hop Songs—a chart that dates to the 1940s—"Uptown Funk!" would have set an all-time record on this chart, with nineteen weeks at No. 1. That would have beaten a pair of prior eighteen-week runs, by Joe Liggins's 1945 hit "The Honeydripper" and Louis Jordan's 1946 topper "ChooChoo Ch'boogie."

Four years after this "Uptown Funk!" decision, *Billboard* made a similar category call regarding Lil Nas X's "Old Town Road." The magazine at first allowed "Road" onto their Hot Country Songs chart, then pulled it off, causing a firestorm in the music industry and accusations of racism in the mainstream media.

One unremarked irony: Lil Nas X's hit was allowed to appear on Hot R&B/Hip-Hop Songs, despite sounding far less like an R&B record than "Uptown Funk!" did. "Road" spent twenty weeks atop Hot R&B/Hip-Hop Songs, giving it the all-time R&B chart record, outlasting Joe Liggins and Louis Jordan.

....

The methodology *Billboard* has been using for its genre charts since 2012 not only led to the exclusionary classification of "Uptown Funk!" It also made the Lil Nas X Country chart controversy, I would argue, inevitable. A beneficial side effect of this controversy was that it turned the subtext of how genre is defined into text, making it plain to the general music-consuming public—which, in turn, made "Old Town Road" a bigger hit. To understand how this happened, one must understand how *Billboard*'s genre charts work.

"Genre is always a blending of both formal structure and cultural context," Oregon State University professor Ehren Pflugfelder told *New Yorker* music critic Amanda Petrusich. "This may be the most frustrating thing about genre for those who want it to be stable over time. What makes something country music is often just as much about what the audience for that genre expects it to be as it is the chord progression, instruments, time signature, or lyrical content...Anyone enthusiastic for the strict adherence to something called genre is engaging in something fundamentally conservative."

Technically, *Billboard*'s niche charts—particularly its R&B/Hip-Hop, Country, and Latin lists—are more format charts than genre charts. As critic and American studies professor Eric Weisbard explains in *Top 40 Democracy: The Rival Mainstreams of American Music*, formats run parallel to but are distinct from genres, which come laden with musical and cultural signifiers: R&B and Adult Contemporary are formats; soul and jazz are genres. Big-*C* Country is a format; small-*c* country is a genre. Weisbard argues that radio and music-business formatting, despite its crass commercial imperatives and often blatant racial essentialism, has been a net plus for both audiences and artists across gender and racial lines—especially in the so-called Rock Era, a period implicitly defined by white, male promulgation of a Black-invented (and to a great extent female-pioneered) art form. However imperfect, formats are walled gardens in which artists just outside the mainstream can innovate and dominate. "The very commercial tendencies that made radio formats, and the music they implanted in our consciousness, suspect aesthetically also made them trailblazers for the sounds, artists, and listeners left out," Weisbard writes.

Ultimately, the audience drives what is acceptable in a radio format. They will tune out if they don't like what they hear, which is unacceptable for an industry driven by, as Weisbard says, "not selling music to listeners [but] selling listeners to advertisers." Audiences have not indicated they're ready to eradicate the idea of the Country or R&B formats, even if these are all fluid concepts—and always have been.

Ergo, an effective genre or format chart—whether R&B, Latin, Country, even Alternative Rock—doesn't track a particular strain of *music*, which can be marked by ever-changing boundaries and ultimately impossible to define. It's meant to track an *audience*. The goal should not be to racially profile consumers of the music—especially with R&B and Country, the two formats most rife with racial essentialism. If an R&B/Hip-Hop chart, for example, tries to cover whatever might be termed soul or rap music, it veers into the subjective, slippery business of determining what, or who, is "Black enough" for the chart. That wouldn't be appropriate for *Billboard*, a purportedly objective arbiter of the music business. However, as the "Uptown Funk!" story illustrates, that's exactly the role they've assigned themselves.

That includes determining what kinds of songs are considered "country enough" for Billboard's flagship Country chart, a determination loaded with cultural baggage. The borders of country are arguably policed more than any other genre—everything from instrumentation to vocal timbre to lyrical content is vetted by gatekeepers, whether industry-sanctioned or self-appointed. Moreover, as Ray Charles's aforementioned best-selling but radio-thwarted foray into the genre showed, racial or cultural identity is also baked into this border-policing. In her book *Black Country Music*, Francesca Royster writes: "Despite shifts in critical and artistic conversations on country music and Blackness, there is still the 'common-sense' idea operating that country music is consummately white in its consumption, production, and sound, and that's reflected in the programming of commercial country radio and the gatekeeping of recognition and labeling by organizations like the Country Music Association and the Grammys."

From the moment *Billboard* started tracking genres, beyond the all-purpose, multigenre "pop" category, it has faced challenges defining their boundaries. The chart now called Hot R&B/Hip-Hop Songs began in 1942 as the Harlem Hit Parade before switching to the regrettable moniker Race Records in 1945. That label came from the music industry, not *Billboard*—much as the industry termed country music "Hillbilly" starting in the 1920s.

Billboard avoided "Hillbilly" when it launched its first country jukebox chart in 1944, going with the confusing—but at least not demeaning—label Folk Records. Five years later, *Billboard* retitled its major genre charts. The Race Records surveys became Rhythm & Blues charts, picking up a term coined by Atlantic Records executive Jerry Wexler. Folk Records became Folk (Country & Western). *Billboard* would drop the Folk tag in 1952 and eliminate the "& Western" by the early '60s.

Once *Billboard* had the chart names established by the '60s, the greater challenge was getting the formula, and the data, underlying each chart right. This was especially challenging for R&B. In the late '50s and early '60s, retailers and radio stations were reporting to *Billboard* all manner of popular songs with even a hint of a beat, by Black or white artists, as R&B. By 1963, this became untenable. In the *Billboard* issue dated November 23, 1963, just under half of the Top 10 on the Hot R&B Singles chart was by white acts, including easy-listening pop tracks "Deep Purple" by Nino Tempo and April Stevens and "I'm Leaving It Up to You" by Dale & Grace; and, at No. 1, "Sugar Shack" by kitschy pop band Jimmy Gilmer & the Fireballs. The rest of the R&B Top 10 did feature hits by Black artists Rufus Thomas, Sam Cooke, and Ray Charles, but none of those songs ever reached No. 1 on the R&B chart. One week after this November '63 chart, *Billboard* pulled the chart and kept it on hiatus for fourteen months. When *Billboard* brought back Hot Rhythm & Blues Singles in January 1965, its No. 1 song was the Temptations' "My Girl," and other than one

Righteous Brothers song, the revamped chart comprised all people of color. The chart formula had been refined: only radio stations specializing in R&B had their reported airplay baked into the new chart—no Top 40 stations or other formats that might play some rhythmic music. As for the record-sales component, the magazine now focused on what it came to call "core R&B stores": retailers, many Black-owned, in cities that sold primarily R&B records to a largely, though not exclusively, Black clientele. In short, the revamped chart wasn't going to track R&B music per se; it was going to track the R&B *audience*.

As for *Billboard*'s Hot Country chart, Nashville, and especially country radio, held greater sway over the boundaries of the format. In the '60s, for example, while certain country singles crossed pop ("Crazy," "King of the Road," "Wichita Lineman," "Harper Valley, P.T.A.," "A Boy Named Sue"), the biggest stars on the Hot Country chart were the likes of Buck Owens, George Jones, and Jim Reeves. As country-pop crossover became more common in the '70s and early '80s—especially after the hit 1980 John Travolta movie *Urban Cowboy*—*Billboard* was compelled to adjust the Hot Country formula to keep it authentic as Nashville defined it.

One issue with *Billboard*'s airplay-plus-sales formula on the country side was that the magazine never developed a "core country" retail model to match its robust "core R&B stores" model. Country singles tended to sell at the same kinds of retailers as pop records—mass merchants, department stores as well as traditional record shops—which made it challenging to prize apart the country audience at the retail counter. (Country singles rarely sold well enough to go gold. When the labels considered cutting out unprofitable vinyl 45s for certain country hits, the loudest complaints came not from consumers but from jukebox operators.) What this meant was that Country chart success was—and still is—driven by radio. That had been historically true about the format ever since Nashville station WSM launched the Grand Ole Opry in 1925. But it only became more entrenched by the '70s and '80s as fans either listened to their favorites on country stations or bought LPs. In January 1987, *Billboard* entirely dropped singles sales as a factor for Hot Country Singles; the chart was now all-radio. Three years later, the magazine even eliminated the requirement that a song be issued as a retail single to chart. This gave radio unfettered power to govern hits in the format—and it helped ensure the Hot Country chart would not be overdetermined by pop crossover, the root of the "Old Town Road" debate decades later.

Both formats, R&B and Country, benefited tremendously from *Billboard*'s switch to computerized tallying (see chapter 4). In 1990, the Hot Country chart was converted from self-reported station playlists to computerized detections via Broadcast Data Systems (BDS). The BDS-fueled Hot Country chart tracked the explosion of a new wave of country stars, including Garth Brooks, Tim McGraw, and Shania Twain. On the sales side, the SoundScan-driven album charts reflected the multiplatinum tonnage these acts were selling. As for R&B, the SoundScan and BDS technologies finally began to reflect the rise of rap as a cultural force, with bigger hits by Dr. Dre and Snoop Dogg, 2Pac and Biggie, Jay-Z and Missy Elliott, as well as the dialogue between hip-hop and R&B by the likes of Mary J. Blige, Lauryn Hill, and D'Angelo.

This period of credible genre tracking began to erode after 2000, undone by the rise of digital music—especially on the R&B/hip-hop side. As I noted in chapter 4, digital downloads—sold primarily by Apple's iTunes Music Store—were baked into the Hot 100 starting in 2005. But *Billboard*, fearful of jeopardizing its core-stores model, did not factor iTunes into the R&B/Hip-Hop chart during the 2000s; only physical singles sales still counted. This became increasingly problematic. The new millennium had been tough on brick-and-mortar music chains such as Tower Records, Coconuts, and Strawberries, and downright brutal on the smaller shops that reported to *Billboard*'s R&B charts, which were disappearing just as quickly. In any case, so few physical singles were being released in the '00s that the remaining Black-owned and -oriented music stores didn't have much singles sales data to report. So, for the most part, during the '00s Hot R&B/Hip-Hop Songs was an all-radio chart; physical singles sales still counted but had an infinitesimal impact. This overreliance on radio made the chart rather hollow. In 2009 and 2010, fewer than ten songs topped the R&B chart all year, as hits by Jamie Foxx, Maxwell, Alicia Keys, Chris Brown, and Beyoncé enjoyed perpetual radio rotation and spent months each at No. 1.

Billboard's Country chart didn't have this issue—it had converted to an all-radio formula back in 1987, and sales weren't even a factor. But by the late '00s, country downloads at iTunes were selling in the millions. Acts like Rascal Flatts, Miranda Lambert, and the Zac Brown Band now had platinum-certified songs, and these sales were being ignored on the Hot Country Songs chart. Country radio gatekeepers ensured that mostly acts that came up through the Nashville system were climbing the charts. Nashville liked it this way. The biggest-selling country downloads weren't by format stalwarts like George Strait, Reba McEntire, or Toby Keith; they were pop crossover singles like Carrie Underwood's "Before He Cheats," Miley Cyrus's "The Climb," or Lady Antebellum's "Need You Now." Letting downloads have too great an impact on the Hot Country chart would have overstated the duration of these tracks with a core country crowd.

The real issue for *Billboard* in the digital era was there was no "Black iTunes" or "country iTunes." Hardcore R&B/hip-hop or country fans generally patronize the same sites to purchase and stream songs as everyone else—in the winner-take-all game of digital music, any format-specific site would get crushed by Apple's iTunes, Google's YouTube, and, by the '10s, Spotify. These digital emporiums' dominance isn't a problem when it comes to the Hot 100, which covers all genres; there, all songs can compete on equal footing. But the whole point of *Billboard*'s R&B and Country charts was to highlight sales and airplay targeted at core genre fans. How can they do that if sales and streams generated by these consumers can't be isolated?

In 2012, *Billboard* in essence punted on this whole question. The magazine announced an overhaul to its R&B/Hip-Hop, Country, and Latin Songs charts, all of which would now begin to incorporate digital sales and streaming. The modernization of these genre charts was long overdue, but *Billboard*'s new methodology was arguably too comprehensive. Now digital sales from any source, any buyer (i.e., mainstream pop fans), would be factored into each chart. *Billboard* also decided that if they were going to count sales from all audiences, they should also track airplay to all audiences, to achieve sales and radio parity. So the new genre charts incorporated airplay across *all* radio formats. Airplay from Top 40 stations of, say, an R&B song would now count for the R&B chart, airplay of a country song would count for the Country chart, and so forth.

In essence, each chart was now a mini–Hot 100. *Billboard* would use the same data providers that fed into the main pop chart for these reconfigured genre charts, and simply trim each chart back to whatever songs the magazine determined fit that genre. They became, in essence, "accordion charts." Here's what I mean: You, the ordinary fan, can compile any week's R&B/Hip-Hop or Country chart yourself. Simply take that week's Hot 100; cross out the songs that aren't R&B/hip-hop or country; and restack all the songs that are left, keeping them in the same order (in my metaphor, squeezing the accordion). Voilà: instant genre chart. This is a crude way to measure genre penetration and consumption. It assumes that everybody in America is an equal fan of all genres. Worse, the new approach largely makes *crossover* as it was originally defined—songs transitioning, over weeks or months, from genre chart to mass audience—impossible, because every week the Hot 100 and the genre charts are, at root, versions of the same chart.

Followers of the genre charts were instantly unhappy. Country fans, protective as ever of their demimonde, were especially aghast. "Foremost, the incorporation of airplay from other formats basically handed control of the top of *Billboard*'s genre-specific songs charts over to programmers of the format that generates the largest audience impressions: CHR/Top 40," country music blogger Devarati Ghosh wrote.[1] The new world order of these pop-driven genre charts was laid bare the very first week of the switch. Taylor Swift, who was in the process of transitioning from country to pop in 2012 with her Max Martin–produced hit "We Are Never Ever Getting Back Together," saw that song shoot from No. 21 to No. 1 on the revamped Hot Country Songs chart, even though "Never Ever" wasn't scoring much airplay on country radio stations. Rihanna, whose singles had long done better

---

1. "Contemporary Hits Radio" (CHR) is another name for what is more colloquially known as Top 40 radio. Since few pop stations actually play forty current records, it's a more all-purpose term.

on pop radio than Black radio, made an even bigger pole vault on Hot R&B/Hip-Hop Songs, from No. 66 to No. 1, with "Diamonds," a song receiving only modest Black radio airplay. Even *Billboard*'s smaller charts weren't immune. Hot Rap Songs, a companion to the R&B/Hip-Hop chart that isolated pure rap output, also had the Hot 100 data set baked into its formula, and rap fans howled when the first No. 1 song on the revamped Hot Rap Songs was K-pop star Psy's viral hit "Gangnam Style."

What is most dubious about this system is how *Billboard*, supposedly an objective chart-maker, is now in the sorry business of deciding who qualifies for each genre chart, with all the questionable implications that come with that identity categorization process. When faced with margin calls, the magazine consults with the labels to see which radio formats they are promoting the song to, and they also assess the sound of the song itself. In other words, *Billboard* now plays a role that used to be played organically—by shoppers at Black retail stores, who collectively decided in 1982 that Hall and Oates' "I Can't Go for That" was a legitimate R&B song, or listeners to country radio, who in 1984 stayed tuned when their stations played Lionel Richie's "Stuck on You."[2] Now *Billboard*'s

---

2. If *Billboard* had employed its modern accordion-style methodology on the Hot Country chart in 1984, Lionel Richie's hit would have hit No. 1 on that chart, thanks to its massive sales and to pop and R&B fans—which would have been a gross overstatement of its embrace by core country fans. The song's actual '84 country peak, No. 24, more accurately reflects how it did with the country audience—a sizable country hit, not a smash.

editors are the ones making the call that Justin Timberlake is acceptable on the R&B/Hip-Hop chart but Bruno Mars isn't, or that certain Post Malone songs are hip-hop. Once *Billboard* makes that call, all of Post's airplay across formats and his massive streams from pop fans pour into the R&B/Hip-Hop chart, misrepresenting the extent of his popularity with R&B/hip-hop fans.

Or . . . the magazine might decide a twangy song by a Black Atlantan in a cowboy hat isn't country music, even though that young man says it is.

....

When Lil Nas X uploaded "Old Town Road" to streaming services like Spotify and Apple Music in the closing weeks of 2018, he labeled it a country song in the track metadata that streaming services use to categorize music. This was pure hustle on Montero Hill's part—he was seeking the widest possible audience for a track that did legitimately sound like country. (He also tagged the song as hip-hop.)

By March 2019, as the song amassed considerable streams thanks to its virality, "Old Town Road" debuted on the Hot 100 at No. 83. Because the song was tagged as country, and the Hot Country Songs chart is just a culled version of the Hot 100, "Road" also debuted there, all the way up at No. 19—notably high for a song from an artist new to country music, particularly one receiving, to that date, zero country radio airplay. But again, given *Billboard*'s "accordion" approach, if there were only eighteen other songs on the Hot 100 that week higher than Lil Nas X's that the magazine considered country, those eighteen songs, in that order, would make up the top 18 on Hot Country Songs—from Luke Combs's "Beautiful Crazy" (No. 25 Hot 100 that week, ergo No. 1 Hot Country) to Kelsea Ballerini's "Miss Me More" (No. 81 Hot 100, No. 18 Hot Country). The 83rd-ranked "Old Town Road" on the Hot 100 therefore ranked 19th at Hot Country.

By letting "Old Town Road" onto the Country chart in the first place, *Billboard* shone a light on what might have been a noncontroversy. The hullabaloo began a week later, when *Billboard* put out its charts for the week ending March 23, 2019, and the magazine had pulled "Old Town Road" from Hot Country Songs. For the record, if they hadn't done that, "Road," which was flying up the Hot 100, would have leapt from No. 19 to No. 3 on the Hot Country chart—then to No. 1 two weeks after that.

Billboard was, in essence, choosing among two bad options their genre methodology forced them into: the bad optics of letting the song stay on the chart, in which case a left-field, country-adjacent song by a first-time artist becomes an instant top three country hit; or the even worse optics of yanking a country hit by a young Black artist, in a genre that already has precious few Black stars. Remarkably, the magazine chose the latter route, reportedly under pressure from Nashville factions (though *Billboard*'s director of charts would later deny there was any undue pressure). A Nashville-based agent revealed to National Public Radio that "part of the pushback against Lil Nas X wasn't just related to race—it was also the country industry being afraid of how the rapper emerged: on social media, without going through the Nashville gatekeepers."

In an official statement, *Billboard* stated that Lil Nas X's song "incorporates references to country and cowboy imagery [but] does not embrace enough elements of today's country music to chart in its current version." *Billboard* later added that their "decision to take the song off of the country chart had absolutely nothing to do with the race of the artist." The statement was repeated and amplified across the mainstream media.

Billboard's own-goal on Lil Nas X did not simply reveal the racism underlying genre designations and the cloistered practices of the Nashville Industrial Complex; it also indicted the fundamental flaws in *Billboard*'s post-2012 genre charts system. That system does not allow country fans to make up their own minds about a song that straddles genres, like "Old Town Road." A methodology that limited itself to country fans' sales, streams, and radio exposure would have allowed the song onto the Country chart but given it a more realistic berth—not instantly debuting at No. 19, which was itself a misrepresentation of its country acceptance.

Ironically, the *Billboard*-vs.–Lil Nas X controversy likely turned the song into a pop smash all by itself. "Old Town Road" instantly went from a meme to a cause. But to begin with it was a meme. And it might have stayed a meme, pinging around the self-reinforcing ecosystem of the interwebs, had the Country chart–

yanking never happened. Before we arrive at the denouement of the "Old Town Road" story—when it becomes a nationwide über-smash—we should consider another parallel universe, one in which "Old Town Road" is remembered as the short-lived cultural by-product of a video game and a Chinese social app.

▶ 06 WORLD WIDE 'til I Can't No More

How Technology and Internet Culture
Built "Old Town Road"

In January 2006, thirteen years before "Old Town Road," the top of the Hot 100 was briefly overtaken by a quartet from the Bankhead Projects, the very same Atlanta housing development where six-year-old Montero Hill was then living. They did it with a quirky track that's arguably the simplest No. 1 song ever. They topped the chart for a week and would never hit the Top 40 again.

"Laffy Taffy" was by D4L, an acronym for Down for Life. Its chorus comprised a finger snap, a three-note synth hook, and an incessantly repeating "Girl, shake that laffy taffy / That laffy taffy." It was a prototypical example of the hip-hop subgenre snap music. An Atlanta-based offshoot of crunk, snap was rap reduced to its digital essence: an 808 thump, a bit of hi-hat, some snapping (of course), and chanting vocals, the simpler the better. Hits in the minigenre included "Snap Yo Fingers" by crunk godfather Lil Jon, "Play" by Mississippi rapper David Banner, and "Lean wit It, Rock wit It" by Atlanta troupe Dem Franchize Boys. Snap's peak in the mid-'00s was a bit like psychedelic rock's in the late '60s, in that it only had a two-to-three-year run but left a mark. The establishment of trap beats in the '00s and '10s—a sound that reshaped rap, to the point that much of modern hip-hop and even pop is built around trap—can be traced to the shorter-lived crunk and snap phenomena.

D4L's "Laffy Taffy" was snap's über-hit. The week it shot from No. 4 to No. 1 on the Hot 100, it unseated Mariah Carey's late 2005 chart-topper "Don't Forget about Us." How exactly did D4L's skeletal hit dethrone the goddess of pop-and-B? In a word, technology.

The 2005 holiday season was the first in which Apple's iTunes Music Store counted for the Hot 100. Apple's iPod was at a peak of gifting popularity. A lot of teenagers woke up on Christmas with a new gadget to fill with songs, and iTunes gift cards in their stockings. They needed software for their hardware—and ninety-nine–cent download buyers made "Laffy Taffy" a smash. The January 2006 chart where D4L went to No. 1 was based on data collected by *Billboard* the week after Christmas: December 26, 2005, through January 1, 2006. For that one week, "Laffy Taffy" sold 175,000 dollar downloads, a record at the time. If not for those thousands of downloads, "Laffy" never would have topped the Hot 100; it was not among radio's fifteen most played songs.

Snap music was also called "ringtone rap," crisp and simple enough to be reproduced by primitive, chirpy '00s mobile phones. (In 2005, Apple's iPhone did not yet exist.) Ringtones were the way candy-bar and flip phones could be customized by users to identify callers. Ringtones were big moneymakers for the recording industry during their short-lived peak. *Billboard* even tracked them on their own Hot Ringtones chart for about a decade (2004–14). While ringtone purchases never counted for the Hot 100, the viral technology had a knock-on effect. The presence of "Laffy Taffy" on scores of Motorola and Nokia phones made the song ubiquitous, compelling thousands to buy the full D4L song, which *did* count for the big chart. During the song's twenty-six-week Hot 100 run, about 3 million Americans bought the full-length "Laffy Taffy."

"Laffy Taffy" could fairly be called the first No. 1 hit powered by mobile virality—consuming it in short bursts compelled millions to want to hear the whole song. In other words, what ringtones were to the mid-'00s, TikTok was to the end of the '10s, blazing a trail toward "Old Town Road."

....

The interplay of music and technology comes in two varieties: the medium and the marketing. As fundamental as technology is to the form music takes, the ways it promotes and socializes music consumption—the conversation *around* the music—may be even more essential.

In terms of medium, technology has long shaped the songs themselves. The common length of a popular song, averaging around three minutes, was driven first by the late nineteenth-century technology of phonograph cylinders, which ran two to four minutes in length, and then, by the 1920s, the development of the ten-inch 78-RPM shellac record, which topped out at three minutes a side. That average length stayed intact through the launch in the late 1940s of the 45-RPM vinyl single, on which sides were ideally no longer than five minutes, although a few hits— like the Beatles' seven-minute 1968 No. 1 "Hey Jude"—were longer. More recently, during the streaming era, songs have gotten shorter, because more repeat song plays on Spotify means higher royalties for artists. "Old Town Road," at 1:53 in its original form, is a quintessential streaming-era single.

As for marketing, there was such a thing as a viral hit before the internet. In 1960 and again in '62, Chubby Checker's "The Twist" became the first-ever single to reach No. 1 in two separate chart runs, as the titular dance spread like an infection from young to old. Its climb to the top in September '60 was fueled by teenagers learning the dance from TV's *American Bandstand*. More than a year later, as photos appeared in the press of clubgoers doing the Twist at places like New York City's Peppermint Lounge, the dance and song were deemed kosher for adults. Checker's "The Twist" reentered the Hot 100 and, by January '62, had climbed back to No. 1. That was about as fast as a viral musical phenomenon could propagate, pre-internet.

The first ever major-label distribution of a song over the internet came in 1994: an Aerosmith B-side, "Head First," issued free by Geffen Records on the consumer internet service provider CompuServe. (It took about ninety minutes to download the four-and-a-half-minute track.) The first song *sold* online came three years later: Duran Duran's minor hit "Electric Barbarella" (No. 52, 1997) was issued by Capitol Records as a ninety-nine-cent digital single. Both of these were essentially beta tests. Aerosmith's track was distributed as a WAV file in fairly low fidelity; the Duran Duran single was sold in a long-defunct format called Liquid Audio. These experiments were nascent attempts to control digital music distribution. A 1994 *New York Times* article about the Aerosmith single noted: "At stake may be nothing less than the future of the record business. If songs are available free through a computer's phone line, this leaves record labels, manufacturers and retailers out in the cold." As for the 1997 Duran Duran single, *Billboard* called the trial "a critical early attempt to establish a legitimate alternative to a little-known phenomenon of music piracy." To that point, no viable high-quality, bandwidth-friendly digital music format existed.

That was about to change, after a team of German engineers pioneered the field of compressed audio with an encoding schema they dubbed "MPEG-1 Audio Layer III," or MP3: a lossy music compression format that achieved passable audio quality in a bandwidth-friendly file size. By 1997, the MP3 began to take hold on college campuses, commonly wired with high-speed internet; and the MP3 was essential to the 1999 success of Napster, which popularized the practice of internet file-sharing and mass-scale electronic musical piracy. This eventually led to the 2003 launch of Apple's iTunes Music Store, when music downloads came of age as ecommerce. By 2005, downloads were woven into *Billboard*'s major chart formulas.

As vital as all these advances were, in hindsight the more profound musical invention of the aughts wasn't file-sharing or even the dollar download; it was social media and video-sharing. In other words, the metanarrative became more vital than the medium. The invention of YouTube, for example, was first inspired by creators who wanted to find a more convenient way to share video of the Justin Timberlake–Janet Jackson wardrobe malfunction from the 2004 Super Bowl halftime show. Within months of YouTube's 2005 launch, music videos were the most viral content, kicking off with the *Saturday Night Live*/Lonely Island parody rap video "Lazy Sunday."

By 2006, years before the music business came up with a model to monetize video-sharing, YouTube was already fueling music consumption, much as MTV had in the 1980s. "Weird Al" Yankovic, the veteran purveyor of comical music and song parodies, scored the first Top 10 hit of his long career in October 2006, the week he turned forty-seven, when "White and Nerdy," his parody of rapper Chamillionaire's "Ridin' (Dirty)" and a YouTube sensation, sold seventy-one thousand downloads in a week and vaulted from No. 28 to No. 9. As with "Laffy Taffy" and the ringtone, Yankovic's video activity, which did not count for the Hot 100, had a knock-on effect on his digital sales. One year after "White and Nerdy," a seventeen-year-old rapper born DeAndre Way, who dubbed himself Soulja Boy Tell 'Em, scored the first No. 1 hit–cum–YouTube dance craze when his video "Crank That (Soulja Boy)" blew up on the site. Soulja Boy was both Way's rap name and the name of his dance, a bounceback-plus–Superman pose maneuver. "Crank That" spent seven weeks atop the Hot 100, fueled by weekly download sales roughly twice the size of D4L's in late '05. The Lonely Island's, Weird Al's, and Soulja Boy's early successes on YouTube—and on then-nascent social media, where all these videos were heavily shared—offered a blueprint for the novelty/comedy-plus-music combination Lil Nas X would pursue in his quest for virality a dozen years later.

In this period, social media was dominated by Myspace, a platform heavily invested in music. The site offered a user-friendly way to upload songs or albums, many hosted on artists' own Myspace pages. UK postpunk band Arctic Monkeys was arguably the first act with a Myspace-fueled chart-topper, when their 2005 debut single "I Bet You Look Good on the Dancefloor" entered the British chart at No. 1; the band professed ignorance of the site and said the Myspace activity was fomented by their fans. In 2009, a Christian electropop artist named Adam Young, who called himself Owl City, replicated the Myspace feat in America, reaching No. 1 on the Hot 100 with his own debut single, "Fire-flies." Unlike Arctic Monkeys, the introverted Young proactively curated his Myspace profile, developing a fanbase that led to his signing with major label Universal Republic. Young's manager told a music-industry blog that the label saw Owl City as "repre-senting the future of our business" and added, "People feel like they know [Owl City], like they've got a direct connection to him because of how he approaches his connection with them online."

In the '10s, as Myspace gave way to Facebook and Twitter, the social era of the charts began in earnest. Female pop stars, in particular, were wizards at using social media to create a simula-crum of fan intimacy. At the peak of Lady Gaga's chart success in 2011, *Rolling Stone* revealed that she was not only Twitter's most-followed music star but the site's most-followed person, period, with a commanding 11 million followers; her Facebook stats were similarly massive, with 39 million "likes" at the time, edging out Rihanna and Shakira. Around the same time, Taylor Swift made expert use of the social apps to stoke engagement with fans, even other artists. A 2014 Instagram video selfie of Swift lip-syncing rapper Kendrick Lamar's "Backseat Freestyle" was heavily shared and played a role in Swift's eventual connection with mutual admirer Lamar, who then provided a featured rap on the remix of her 2015 No. 1 hit "Bad Blood."

YouTube also came of age as a music influencer at the turn of the '10s. It took until 2009 for the record business to find a way to monetize YouTube, with the launch of Vevo, an industry-sponsored all–music video site that leveraged YouTube's video-hosting technology and advertising platform. Around the same time, Canadian adolescent Justin Bieber was discovered via You-Tube, signing a contract with Island Def Jam at age fourteen. In 2010, the then-fifteen-year-old Bieber's video for "Baby" became the first YouTube video of any kind to break half a billion views. Though the song received only modest airplay on tween-averse Top 40 radio stations, "Baby" sold 4 million copies to video-besotted fans and reached No. 5 on the Hot 100.

Bieber paid it forward a couple of years later, giving a boost to fellow Canadian pop singer Carly Rae Jepsen by talking up her irresistible confection "Call Me Maybe" on Twitter. When Jepsen dropped the "Maybe" video on YouTube, the song blew up in America, debuting on the Hot 100 in March and hitting No. 1 by June. What made the song viral wasn't just its official video—a suburban daydream in which Jepsen pines for a local boy who, in a final twist, might turn out to prefer men. It was also a swarm of viral user videos. Scores of users uploaded lip-dubs and covers of "Call Me Maybe" to YouTube, including members of the 2012 US Olympic team and an array of *Sesame Street* Muppets. These viral videos did not have any direct chart impact—through the end of 2012, *Billboard* still did not count YouTube views for the Hot 100. The knock-on effects on traditional sales and airplay were significant, however.

A major 2012 test of YouTube's hitmaking prowess was "Gangnam Style" by Psy, a South Korean pop-rapper whose signature song was a sly satire of materialistic East Asian consumerism. The "Gangnam Style" video, which featured Psy doing a comical horsey-riding dance—yet another "Old Town Road" precursor—was the first YouTube video to surpass 1 billion views worldwide. That spurred sales of more than 5 million downloads in America, which, in turn, spurred terrestrial radio airplay. At its peak, "Gangnam" ranked 12th on *Billboard*'s weekly Radio Songs chart—remarkable, given the song's 98 percent Korean lyrics—and it was America's top-selling download for more than a month. Had YouTube views counted for the Hot 100 then, Psy would have had K-Pop's first-ever US chart-topper, eight years ahead of blockbuster Korean boy band BTS. Instead, given its impressive but still limited radio spins, "Gangnam" peaked at No. 2 on the Hot 100 for seven weeks in the fall of 2012.

Carly Rae Jepsen's and Psy's 2012 hits just missed *Billboard*'s addition of YouTube data to the charts, which happened early the next year. Starting with the Hot 100 dated March 2, 2013, *Billboard* factored in not only plays of label-sanctioned videos on Vevo but also fan videos incorporating at least half a minute of an original recording. This led to yet another important precedent for "Old Town Road": the first internet meme to directly create a No. 1 hit. The week *Billboard* made its YouTube rule change, a song that hadn't been on the Hot 100 the prior week—and had little radio airplay and only modest download sales—suddenly materialized atop the chart: "Harlem Shake," a trap-style club record by EDM producer Harry Rodrigues, who went by *nom de deejay* Baauer. Baauer's largely instrumental track had become a viral phenomenon, taking a starring role in a video meme in which gangs of costumed young people pelvic-thrusted their way through the song. What made "Harlem Shake" an instant smash wasn't an official video by Baauer; he didn't even have a fully produced video, only a bare-bones clip of the track playing over the single's artwork. "Shake" instead benefited largely from *Billboard*'s new fan-video rule. The week the track hit No. 1, it was heard in YouTube videos 103 million times, mostly viral fan videos. (This streaming record would later be broken by Lil Nas X.) Baauer never had another Hot 100 hit.

Later in 2013, an established act, Disney Channel refugee–turned–pop provocateur Miley Cyrus, benefited just as profoundly from the YouTube rule as Baauer but also showed the potential of nascent social-video apps. Cyrus went to No. 1 with her torch ballad "Wrecking Ball," fueled—at first—by her official, label-issued video featuring a naked Cyrus riding an actual iron ball. The clip tallied nearly 40 million YouTube views in its first week, propelling the song to the top of the Hot 100 before it had even become a radio hit. Nine weeks after "Ball" fell out of No. 1, it went back to the top for one more week fueled not by the official clip but by an affectionate video lampoon of the song from a fan named Stephen Kardynal. He posted a supercut video of himself, wearing just his underwear and a bushy beard, lip-syncing "Wrecking Ball" on a ball à la Cyrus to unsuspecting users of Chatroulette, a then-novel video-chat service. Kardynal's You-

Tube compilation captured Chatrouletters' delighted but flabbergasted reactions on one side of the screen while he rode his ball and sang on the other side. Because Kardynal's clip used the original audio of Cyrus's hit, its views counted for the Hot 100. For the chart week of December 14, 2013, *Billboard* reported that more than half of "Wrecking Ball's" 18 million streams were for Kardynal's video. That was enough to push "Ball" back to No. 1 on the Hot 100.

Chatroulette's first wave of popularity was fairly short-lived (the service later made a comeback during the COVID-19 pandemic). Between the launches of Chatroulette and TikTok came Vine, a short-form video service launched in 2012 and acquired by Twitter, on which users shared six-second-long, looping clips. In its scant four years of existence—2013 to 2017—Vine spun off a colossal number of micromemes: from "on fleek," a catchphrase coined by user Peaches Monroee to describe her eyebrow job; to six-year-old Terrance Jackson simply saying the name "LeBron James" several times in a specific cadence. Jackson's "LeBron James" became so famous that it was invoked in a school-assembly scene in the 2018 Bo Burnham film *Eighth Grade*, capturing how deeply the meme had penetrated Generation-Z culture.

Early in the life of Vine, the service created a hit song fueled by a viral dance, invented by a Jamaican American rapper, Ackquille Pollard, who called himself Bobby Shmurda. "Hot Boy"—original title: "Hot N***a"—began its life as a full-length, homemade video of the nineteen-year-old Schmurda drinking, smoking, and performing his single on a street in Brooklyn surrounded by friends. The key moment in the video—around the 2:20 mark, when Shmurda pops off his Knicks cap, turns his back to the camera, and does a side-to-side hip swivel with back and arm twists—was isolated by a Vine user in June 2014 as the "Shmoney Dance." That Vine clip was watched more than 3 million times in two months, during which Shmurda signed with Epic Records. In August 2014, the song (serviced by the label in a more radio-friendly "Hot Boy" edit) broke on the Hot 100, and by October it had cracked the Top 10, fueled largely by YouTube exposure; it peaked at No. 6. Viral dances turned out to be Vine's killer app—hundreds of Vine users uploaded their own six-second takes on the Shmoney Dance. The following year, Ricky Hawk, a seventeen-year-old Atlanta rapper who went by Silentó, dropped the track "Watch Me (Whip/Nae Nae)" with its own signature dance on Sound-Cloud, YouTube, Instagram, and Vine. Only the YouTube activity counted for the Hot 100, but that was enough to propel "Watch Me" to No. 3 by July 2015.

By the time Twitter shut Vine down in January 2017 (the site was largely done in by Instagram, which co-opted its microvideo format in its new "Instagram Stories"), a competitor-cum-successor was already on the rise. Chinese company ByteDance had launched a short-video service, Douyin, aimed at a domestic Chinese audience in 2016. Douyin rapidly scaled to 100 million users, but ByteDance decided they would need to relaunch the app to compete globally. So in 2017 they launched a Western

Hemisphere–targeted global version—really, a parallel video eco-system separate from Douyin—branded as TikTok. Unlike Vine, whose videos were a strict six seconds, TikTok permitted clips of a languid fifteen seconds. (Minute-long clips were later permitted.) One other killer feature of TikTok was its music integration; the app made it exceptionally easy for video creators to sync up songs to their creations. And TikTok's gamelike interface—it threads videos thematically, such that one follows another in a kind of stack—made the app extremely addicting.

Just months after the launch, ByteDance affirmed their latest creation's music-driven personality by acquiring Musical.ly, a lip-syncing selfie-video service popular with Western tweens and teens, and merging it into TikTok. The elimination of the Musical.ly brand and the porting of its roughly 200 million users to TikTok was complete by August 2018—around the time Montero Hill was bouncing between his tweetdeck personas and beginning to record as Lil Nas X. He took notice of the rapid growth of TikTok and began exploring it as another platform for his viral conquest. Hill could see that the app was emerging as the most powerful meme-generator since Vine and ramping up quickly. In the month of September 2018, *Business Insider* later reported, TikTok was the most-downloaded app in the United States.

What transpired next was a mix of market savvy and happenstance. Both Lil Nas X and TikTok happened to catch a moment when a specific meme was bubbling to the surface on social media, mixing an intersectional fashion conversation crossed with a megapopular video game.

In late September 2018, one year after rapper Young Thug's *Beautiful Thugger Girls* mixtape caught some attention for the "Yee-haw!" that led off "Family Don't Matter" (see chapter 3), R&B singer Ciara tweeted a photo shoot of herself in western wear, appearing on the fall cover of fashion magazine *King Kong*. That same day, a Texan Twitter user named Bri Malandro tweeted a pair of the Ciara photos with an appended caption: "the yee haw agenda is in full effect." Malandro later told *Jezebel* that she meant nothing deep by the tweet, that "it was 1,000 percent supposed to be fun … It's a play on 'the gay agenda.' My mind works in mysterious ways, and it kind of just came to me." (She would later apply for a trademark on the term.)

Regardless of Malandro's modest quest for Twitter attention, the phrase *Yeehaw Agenda* took on a life of its own. It seemed to limn a conversation around the history of the Black cowboy that had been percolating through various media over the prior two years. These included a widely shared 2017 *Smithsonian* magazine article, "The Lesser-Known History of African-American Cowboys." And, much more widely, there was the raging debate surrounding the 2016 performance on the CMA Awards by Beyoncé, joined by country trio the Chicks, of her Texas-celebrating, country-and-western-indebted "Daddy Lessons" ("With his right hand on his rifle / He swore it on the Bible / Oh, my daddy said shoot").

A month after Ciara's and Malandro's tweets, Rockstar Games released its blockbuster *Red Dead Redemption 2*, the latest immersive installment in its long-running *Red Dead* franchise of western-themed games. RDR2 arrived in late October 2018 to $725 million in sales in its opening weekend, making it the second-highest launch in gaming history after Rockstar's own *Grand Theft Auto V*. The game received positive press attention for its critique of white supremacy, positive portrayals of Black characters in the Old West, and gamers' ability to exact justice against Ku Klux Klansmen. Given the unsurprising overlap between TikTok users and *Red Dead* players, RDR2 memes quickly sprouted up on the video site, mostly involving game-addled players imitating the grizzled accent of the game's protagonist, Arthur Morgan.

To this point, TikTok was a self-reinforcing ecosystem driven by joke memes and only beginning to show potential as a platform for musical discovery. Songs made famous within the platform weren't yet becoming chart hits outside it. For example, a 2018 track by rap duo iLoveFriday, "Mia Khalifa," took off as a TikTok meme riffing on one of its lyrics, "Hit or miss, I guess they never miss, huh?," but the deliberately amateurish song never appeared on a *Billboard* chart. "Old Town Road" changed all that, as the first song-plus-meme-plus-Zeitgeist-shifter truly incubated on TikTok. Within weeks of its release, it was swept up in both the mania for RDR2 and the Yeehaw Agenda.

On December 2, 2018, Lil Nas X released the song on You-Tube in the form of an "official" music video composed entirely of *RDR2* game footage. The next day, he put it out on Spotify and other streaming services. To highlight the song's funniest, most meme-worthy line, Nas posted the song on several platforms with the title "Old Town Road (I Got the Horses in the Back)." In a bit of clever sock-puppetry, on a Reddit page devoted to helping people identify catchy songs, Nas posted, "What's the name of the song that goes 'take my horse to the old town road'?"

The song worked especially well on TikTok, where users keyed into the juncture in the song right after the opening chorus, when the trap beat drops and Nas first sings, "I got the horses in the back." Michael Pelchat, a twenty-one-year-old TikTok star "influencer" who goes by the handle @nicemichael, was (he later claimed) Lil Nas X's Patient Zero—the first to post "Old Town Road" on TikTok, over a fifteen-second clip of himself doing a hoedown-style kick-dance in boots in his Lowell, Massachusetts, bedroom. "It went fuckin' crazy," he later told the *New York Times*. "Everyone was dressed like a cowboy for, like, three weeks."

By the middle of December, a hashtagged #YeehawChallenge had sprouted up, in which clip-makers transformed them-selves from mundane video subjects to fashionable cowboys—usually with a jump, and sometimes with a swig from a cup labeled "YEE YEE JUICE"—at the moment the beat drops and Nas delivers his "got the horses in the back" declaration. Teens, adults, dogs, and cats—all were transformed into would-be cowpokes by a sip of Yee Yee Juice and a jump in the air. Around the holidays, "Old Town Road" gained traction on both SoundCloud—its popularity as a series of fifteen-second video memes was leading people back to the original recording—and Twitter. In a sign of the song's rapid cultural penetration, on December 30, sports site *Bleacher Report* acknowledged the Indianapolis Colts' playoff berth by tweeting a four-second viral video—a mockup of quarterback Andrew Luck standing on the back of a galloping horse—with "Old Town Road" playing underneath.

As 2019 began, Lil Nas X's "Old Town Road" was fully established across social media as the Yeehaw Agenda's official soundtrack. What was mutually reinforcing about the Agenda and the #YeehawChallenge was the broadening of the Black-cowboy cultural discussion into both a meme and a kind of social movement. Roughly a month into the new year, the video meme would accelerate, after an art and fashion critic tweeted a photo that sent the Agenda into the stratosphere (see chapter 7). But even before that happened, "Old Town Road" was already emerging as a wellspring of both social-media mirth and Black cultural pride.

Its journey as a hit song, though, was only just beginning.

▶07 BESTRIDE 'til I Can't No More

How Lil Nas X Dominated 2019

MONTERO LAMAR HILL'S 2019, the year that would turn out to be the biggest of his young life, arguably began in earnest in early December 2018, with two clairvoyant tweets.

On December 2, 2018, the day before he dropped "Old Town Road" on the major music-streaming sites, Hill teased the song's rollout. The veteran Twitter savant, formerly known as @NasMaraj and @NasMarai, now mostly used his @LilNasX handle, which he gave the cheeky display name "nope." His teaser tweet for the new song set the tone: a twenty-nine-second video of a remarkably limber rodeo cowboy, dancing with almost manic swagger.

Whatever the cowpoke was originally dancing to, he was now furiously wiggling and two-stepping to "Old Town Road."

On that tweet, Lil Nas X's caption simply read: "country music is evolving."

Then, on December 4, 2018—one day *after* the drop, as the song was building buzz and already beginning to blow up—Lil Nas X tweeted a wish into the universe. He posted another microvideo, this time a fourteen-second selfie of him lip-syncing his own song in a hoodie, with extreme sangfroid, looking coolly accomplished but a bit lonely.

The caption for that tweet: "twitter please help me get billy ray cyrus on this."

These two tweets—whose captions would both come true in 2019—served as a starter's pistol for perhaps the most improbable couch-surfing-to-Grammy-winning journey in pop chart history. Let's recap it in the historical present, week by week, milestone by milestone.

JANUARY 26, 2019: In the depths of this week's *Billboard* magazine, on the Social 50—a chart that ranks artists based purely on online mentions and shows nothing more than their names and their record labels—a new name debuts at No. 31. The chart entry reads as follows:

NEW	31	**LIL NAS X** UNSIGNED

This is, quite literally, Lil Nas X's first ink in *Billboard* magazine—and an indication of his status as a self-released, self-powered musical persona.

Launched in 2010, the Social 50 ranks artists (not songs or albums) based on virality, by tallying mentions across such social sites as YouTube, Vevo, Facebook, Twitter, Instagram, Sound-Cloud, Vine (while it existed), and Tumblr. TikTok is too new to be a Social 50 component in 2019—but Lil Nas X's penetration of social media via the #YeehawChallenge at this point is so thoroughgoing that his YouTube, SoundCloud, and Twitter activity is more than enough to get him on the chart.

Nas falls off the Social 50 the next week and doesn't return to the pages of *Billboard* until March. By that time, the viral meme that got him into the magazine has grown far bigger.

FEBRUARY 2, 2019: The Yeehaw Agenda meme Bri Malandro instigated the previous fall reaches a new culmination when Brooklyn-based art curator and critic Antwaun Sargent tweets a photo of two shirtless Black male models—one wearing a cowboy hat, the other taking a selfie. His tweet demands, "I need a fashion piece about how the black yeehaw agenda is chic and thriving."

This Sargent tweet is the head of a long Twitter thread comprising photos of striking Black people in cowboy garb: from models dressed by cutting-edge Black fashion designers, to celebrities like Lil Kim, Mary J. Blige, Diana Ross, and Beyoncé in western wear. The thread sprouts more than four hundred responses, many featuring further pictorial contributions. Sargent's call to arms draws responses from both academics and the fashion industry, as well as piles of glossy photos. "As others clamored to add their own pictures to Sargent's chain," writes *Pitchfork*'s Michelle Kim, "it became clear: this archive of Black cowboys and cowgirls wasn't just beautiful. To many, it was a revelation."

All during February and March, this maturation of the Yeehaw Agenda further fuels TikTok's #YeehawChallenge. Videos featuring Lil Nas X's "Old Town Road" explode that month. By the end of March, *Time* reports, videos with the #yeehaw hashtag—thousands of them, almost all soundtracked by "Road"—have been watched more than 67 million times.

MARCH 5, 2019: Fueled by the Yeehaw Agenda's February explosion and another wave of social mentions, Lil Nas X reenters the Social 50 at No. 35—his second time in *Billboard*, on a chart dated March 9, 2019.[1] "Old Town Road," however, is still not on any *Billboard* song charts.

---

1. Throughout this chapter, I will reference both the dates when Billboard reveals its charts—Tuesdays on their website, with major Hot 100 highlights previewed in a Monday news story—and the *official* dates of those charts, which are always the following Saturday. Note that each chart captures data collected much earlier. For example, a Hot 100 dated March 9 is based on digital consumption (streams and downloads) captured in a Friday-to-Thursday window that started fifteen days earlier, on February 22, and that ended six days later, February 28. Radio is on a slightly different tracking week, from Monday to Sunday; so for a March 9–dated chart, radio spins were collected from February 25 through March 3. For more detail on what I call the *Billboard* charts' "data lag," listen to my December 2020 *Hit Parade* episode, the "Smells like Christmas Spirit Edition."

The day before *Billboard* updates its charts for the week, on Instagram, "Old Town Road" gets its first endorsement by a mainstream country star. Brian Kelly of Florida Georgia Line—the country duo who, as noted in a prior chapter, crossed between the country and pop charts in collaboration with rapper Nelly—gives "Road" his seal of approval in an Instagram story with a two-word review: "Big mood."

MARCH 12, 2019: A major week for "Old Town Road," as the song makes its first-ever chart appearances. On the *Billboard* surveys for the week ending March 16, the song's record company is shown as "NOT LISTED"—ongoing evidence that Lil Nas X remains unsigned. This lack of a label means the song isn't being furnished to radio stations and hence has no airplay data yet. A couple of weeks later, a *Rolling Stone* article reveals that DJs were taping "Old Town Road" off YouTube, from the *Red Dead Redemption 2* supercut video Lil Nas X issued himself. They were trying to get it on the air to remain on-trend with the latest social phenomenon.

What's seemingly historic about the chart debut of "Road" is the trifecta of charts it appears on, all in the same week. On the Hot 100, "Road" debuts at No. 83, fueled by streams (up a whopping 302 percent from the prior week) and downloads (up 295 percent). This data factors into whatever genre charts *Billboard* permits the song to appear on, and for that week, it also debuts on both Hot R&B/Hip-Hop Songs at No. 36 and, notably, Hot Country Songs at No. 19, a remarkably high debut for a country newcomer.

In theory—with the caveat that these genre charts now operate under radically different formulas than they used to—this makes "Old Town Road" the first single to chart pop, R&B, and country simultaneously since "We Are the World" in 1985.

Interestingly, in a standalone article tracking the chart debut by social media's hottest new artist, *Billboard* only calls attention to two of these chart positions, the Hot 100 and Hot R&B/Hip-Hop debuts, with no mention of the Hot Country debut. Perhaps the magazine is telegraphing what it is about to do the next week.

MARCH 16, 2019: Remember Lil Nas X's early December tweet, his very public wish for a Billy Ray Cyrus remix? Ron Perry, an executive at Columbia Records—the Sony Music label that's days away from signing Lil Nas X—saw it. He reaches out to Billy Ray's wife, Tish Cyrus, saying that he would love it if Billy Ray heard "Old Town Road" ASAP. On Saturday, March 16, he hears the song for the first time, over morning coffee with Tish. "I actually stood up outta my chair," Cyrus later recalls for the *New York Times*. "I go, 'God, I love that—that dude is *original*.'"

Billy Ray Cyrus knows a thing or two about musical novelty. It's an open question which song title will appear first in his obituary someday: "Old Town Road" or "Achy Breaky Heart." That line-dance country smash from 1992—spawner of the Achy Breaky, the viral dance craze of its day—reached No. 1 on the Country chart and a remarkable No. 4 on the Hot 100 (at a time when country mega-stars like Garth Brooks and Wynonna Judd were selling truck-loads of albums but not crossing to the pop chart with any of their singles). In 1992, the hunky, mulleted, muscle-T-wearing Cyrus sold 9 million copies of his debut album *Some Gave All.*

By early 2019, however, Cyrus is less famous for "Achy Breaky Heart" than for whom he's related to—his daughter, former kids' TV actress and now pop megastar Miley Cyrus. Indeed, Lil Nas X knew who Billy Ray was only because in the late '00s the elder Cyrus played a supporting role on Miley's hit sitcom *Hannah Montana.* It was on the Disney Channel when Montero was about seven years old. "[Lil Nas X] told me the reason he reached out to me was because he said I was the only country dude that he knew, because of *Hannah Montana,*" Cyrus later tells *Business Insider.* "So you really can't question God's plan."

The same weekend, at Columbia Records' invitation, Billy Ray and Tish show up at LA studio the Record Plant for a songwriting session. In twenty minutes with Black songwriter Jocelyn "Jozzy" Donald, Cyrus helps create a new verse and then records it over a guide vocal from Jozzy:

> *Hat down, crosstown, livin' like a rockstar*
> *Spent a lot of money on my brand-new guitar*
> *Baby's got a habit: diamond rings and Fendi sports bras*
> *Ridin' down Rodeo in my Maserati sports car*
> *Got no stress, I've been through all that*
> *I'm like a Marlboro Man, so I kick on back*
> *Wish I could roll on back to that Old Town Road*
> *I wanna . . . riiiide 'til I can't no more*

The new verse will be the signature element of the remix, and Cyrus's husky, weathered, sly, and even slightly syncopated vocal is letter-perfect. Three days later, on March 19, the label asks Cyrus back to the studio, by himself, this time to sing every part of Lil Nas X's composition in case they want to do a full-duet mix. Cyrus gamely records multiple takes in a range of voices, at one point even imitating Johnny Cash. On the final remix—which a Record Plant engineer is furiously working on through the end of March—the first voice heard is Cyrus's, before Lil Nas X starts singing about the horses in the back, making the song sound "more country" from the jump.

This mix choice is deliberate, because the same week Billy Ray Cyrus finishes his vocals, *Billboard* announces that Columbia has signed Lil Nas X . . . and, privately, gives the label some bad news.

MARCH 19, 2019: *Billboard* posts a new set of charts, for the week ending March 23—and "Old Town Road" is on the move. On the Hot 100, the song moves up thirty-two spots to No. 51 in its second week. On the Hot R&B/Hip-Hop Songs chart, it's moving up ten notches to No. 26. On the Hot Country chart, it's moving . . . off entirely.

Billboard informs Lil Nas X's new label that the inclusion of "Old Town Road" on Hot Country Songs "was a mistake," an anonymous insider later tells *Rolling Stone*. The song's prior week on the Country chart, at No. 19, would be its first and its last. The magazine tries to remove the song from the Country chart, and notify Columbia, quietly. It won't be quiet for long.

MARCH 23, 2019: Notorious country-industry pundit / gadfly Kyle "Trigger" Coroneos, outspoken writer of the blog *Saving Country Music*, posts about "Old Town Road" before the ink on *Billboard*'s latest issue is even dry. The self-dubbed Trigger praises the observed absence of "Road" from the new Hot Country chart and implies that the bigotry is Montero Hill's, not Nashville's:

"Old Town Road" is no more country than The Beastie Boys' "High Plains Drifter." Including Wild West signifiers or references to horses in no way qualifies a rap song with a trap beat as country. Furthermore, Lil Nas X is not professing to be a country artist. He's not signed to a country label, and has no affiliation to the country industry whatsoever. Lil Nas X has no ties to the greater Nashville music campus in any capacity. There are no country artists guesting on the track like you had with Bebe Rexha's collaboration with Florida Georgia Line's "Meant To Be." There appears to be absolutely no credible reason to include this song on a country chart aside from a bigoted stereotype bred from the fact that horses and cowboy hats are referenced in the lyrics.

MARCH 24, 2019: Justin Bieber endorses "Old Town Road" on Instagram: "This shit bangs."

MARCH 26, 2019: As *Billboard* posts new charts showing "Old Town Road" still hurtling upward in its third chart week (No. 32 pop, No. 13 R&B/Hip-Hop), *Rolling Stone* reporter Elias Leight publishes a piece titled "Lil Nas X's 'Old Town Road' Was a Country Hit. Then Country Changed Its Mind." Sourced with unnamed industry insiders afraid of upsetting either the chart gods or the Nashville gods, the exposé details how exactly the song wound up on Hot Country Songs before it got yanked: Nas's posting of "Road" to SoundCloud, iTunes, and elsewhere tagged "country" in the first place, combined with the song's rapid acceleration in streams and sales, caught the business off guard. As a result, the week of March 16, when "Road" amassed enough streams and downloads to register on *Billboard*'s charts, the music-biz bible dutifully allowed it onto the Country chart, as labeled, before realizing its "mistake."

What makes *Rolling Stone*'s article go nuclear, however—linked to and cited across not just the music press but also the mainstream media—is a now-infamous statement *Billboard* provides to Leight:

> Upon further review, it was determined that "Old Town Road" by Lil Nas X does not currently merit inclusion on Billboard's country charts. When determining genres, a few factors are examined, but first and foremost is musical composition. While "Old Town Road" incorporates references to country and cowboy imagery, it does not embrace enough elements of today's country music to chart in its current version.

After the initial publication of Leight's story, a *Billboard* representative provides follow-up clarification, first to the lyrics site Genius, that race did not play a part in their decision to remove "Old Town Road" from the Country chart. But *Rolling Stone*'s original "not…enough elements of today's country" statement is what leads coverage everywhere.

Critics outside Nashville's orbit take to their keyboards. *Pitchfork*'s Sheldon Pearce concludes: "It isn't just that the rules are unclear, it's that they seem entirely made up—which they are. *Billboard*'s chart policies are decided by humans and subject to change at any time…When listeners can recognize a rap song's country bonafides, the least that gatekeepers can do is not block its crossover." In the *New Yorker*, Carrie Battan goes further, calling for "the overdue death of genre" and questioning the very purpose of format-based charts: "This kind of semantic hair-splitting, both by *Billboard* and by audiences, misses the point altogether. It's an attempt to preserve a system of genres that has been crumbling for many years, and to affirm the primacy of a chart structure that is no longer relevant." At *The Ringer*, Lindsay Zoladz sagely wonders whether the song "is some kind of cosmic litmus test to determine whether we can still enjoy things." She writes: "If *Billboard* and the *Saving Country Music* ilk wanted to stop 'Old Town Road' in its tracks, they could not have picked a worse tactic than pulling it from the charts, which only drew more attention to the whole debacle."

Zoladz's most prescient statement: "Amid justifiable cries of racism, 'Old Town Road' suddenly became a digital *cause célèbre*." Indeed, this is the moment that changes the commercial fate of "Old Town Road"—when it goes from a meme to a cause. Rarely does a semantic debate among critics or industry insiders cause a cultural product to go supernova. But as word spreads of the own-goal by *Billboard*—as everyone from morning-show radio DJs to evening newscasters to TikTokkers joins the debate over whether "Road" is country music—the public, outside of certain country and Nashville partisans, is clearly on Lil Nas X's side. They are going to make him a chart-topper, no matter what the music-biz bible or the Nashville Industrial Complex thinks of his song.

Plus, like Bieber said the week before, this shit bangs.

MARCH 29, 2019: Lil Nas X is the special guest at State Farm Arena for an Atlanta Hawks basketball game, where he dances to "Old Town Road" with the team's cheerleaders. "He's got the No. 1 song on Spotify!" the Hawks' announcer declares. "And he's in the house tonight—please welcome Atlanta's own Lil Nas X!" Soon, Spotify isn't the only place Nas will be No. 1.

MARCH 30, 2019: Lil Nas X sits for an interview with *Time* magazine's Andrew Chow. Asked to comment on the implied racism, or at least outsider-phobia, of his song's removal from Hot Country Songs, Montero muses, diplomatically, "I believe whenever you're trying something new, it's always going to get some kind of bad reception. For example, when rap started, or when rock and roll began. But with country trap, I in no way want to take credit for that. I believe Young Thug would be one of the biggest pioneers in that."

"The song is country trap," Lil Nas X tells Chow, who questions why it's off the Country chart but still on the R&B/Hip-Hop chart. "It's not one, it's not the other. It's both. It should be on both."

APRIL 3, 2019: Though Billy Ray Cyrus's agreement to record an "Old Town Road" remix actually predates *Billboard*'s removal of the original recording from Hot Country Songs, he is now all in on the campaign to defend the song's country bona fides and has begun teasing the rumored remix on social media. The prior week, Cyrus's management has him cryptically post on Instagram: "Don't try and think inside the box. Don't think outside the box. Think like there is no box. #HorsesInTheBack"

On April 3, on Twitter, Cyrus is more pointed and more personal, alluding in his tweet to his own difficulties, circa "Achy Breaky Heart," with the Nashville establishment. "@LilNasX, Been watching everything going on with OTR. When I got thrown off the charts, Waylon Jennings said to me 'Take this as a compliment'... means you're doing something great! Only Outlaws are outlawed. Welcome to the club!"

APRIL 5, 2019: At midnight Friday, the "Old Town Road" remix drops. With Billy Ray's new verse, the song's length has grown by nearly 40 percent, from 1:53 to 2:37. Lil Nas X celebrates by retweeting his December 4 microvideo and "twitter please help me get billy ray cyrus on this" message with a simple addendum: "it happened !!!"

Critics hail the remix, not only for its seamless blend of Cyrus's and Hill's vocals and styles but also for its implied challenge to the Nashville establishment. The *New York Times*' headline pointedly reads: "Lil Nas X Added Billy Ray Cyrus to 'Old Town Road.' Is It Country Enough for *Billboard* Now?" Coverage across the media, from CNN to *USA Today*, shines the brightest spotlight yet on Montero Hill's country-trap creation, auguring a major chart boost.

But, a key detail: because of the data lag on *Billboard*'s charts, the Cyrus remix's impact won't be apparent for a week and a half—two Hot 100s from now. At this moment, only the original 1:53 mix, credited to Lil Nas X alone, is still charting. For the week ending April 6, "Old Town Road" is up seventeen places on the Hot 100, at No. 15, and it cracks the R&B/Hip-Hop Top 10 at No. 7. For one more week after that, whatever Lil Nas X does chartswise, he will achieve on his own.

APRIL 8, 2019: In its first four weeks, chart-watchers had to wait to learn "Old Town Road"'s fate until Tuesday, the day *Billboard* updates all the charts on its website. This week, *Billboard* posts a story about "Road" on a Monday, because the song just made major chart news. The headline: "Lil Nas X's 'Old Town Road' Leaps to No. 1 on *Billboard* Hot 100." It's the day before Montero Hill's twentieth birthday. Several news stories point out that this is a pretty awesome present.

On the new set of charts that will be dated April 13, 2019, "Old Town Road" leaps all the way from No. 15 to No. 1, on massive gains in all three Hot 100 components. Streams are up 60 percent, its download sales surge by 83 percent, and airplay—a couple of weeks after radio stations finally received an official Columbia single to play—is up 190 percent. Because the Hot R&B/Hip-Hop Songs chart is just a mini–Hot 100, the song leaps to the top there too. And again, this is all for "Road" v1.0. The artist credit atop the charts simply reads: "Lil Nas X."

The news is a delight not just for Lil Nas X and his growing army of TikTok fans but also for chart mavens, as it achieves a pile of unusual feats. *Billboard* reports that Lil Nas X has made "the swiftest ascent to No. 1 on the Hot 100 for an act with no prior Hot 100 history at all, since Baauer blasted in at the top spot with . . . 'Harlem Shake' in March 2013." Its songwriting credit—which Columbia only straightened out with *Billboard* after it signed Nas, correcting the magazine's "NOT LISTED" fine print—includes Trent Reznor, giving the Nine Inch Nails leader his first credit on a No. 1 song. Finally—in a sign of how form follows function and how the '10s era of the stream is akin to the '60s era of the 45—the 1:53-running "Road" is the shortest No. 1 song in fifty-four years, since the 1:49-running "I'm Henry VIII, I Am" by Herman's Hermits in 1965. (On the all-time shortest-song list, "Road" ranks fifth, tied with David Rose's 1962 No. 1 "The Stripper." The very shortest, to this day, is Maurice Williams & the Zodiacs' 1960 topper "Stay," a wisp of a single at just 1:38.)

APRIL 9, 2019: One day after announcing "Road"'s triumph, *Billboard* posts an intriguing follow-up headlined "Lil Nas X's 'Old Town Road' Debuts on Country Airplay, Driven by Morning Show Spins."

As I discussed in chapter 5, Country Airplay is what Hot Country Songs used to be—an all-country-radio chart with no streaming, download, or Top 40 radio data skewing it toward pop-leaning country records. It's regarded by Nashville and chart followers as a barometer of songs' acceptance by actual country fans. Sure enough, "Road" appears on Country Airplay at No. 53. Though commentators outside Nashville make hay that, after shunning the song, country gatekeepers now seem to be reluctantly embracing it, *Billboard*'s story reveals the spins are more out of curiosity than audience traction: "Almost all plays for 'Road' in the latest tracking week occurred during morning drive, thanks to syndicated plays on *The Bobby Bones Show*. Although one station . . . WMAD Madison, Wis., played it 14 times . . . no other [station] gave it more than five plays."

So core country listeners, like the rest of America, are consuming "Old Town Road" as much for the metaconversation as for the song itself. Unlike pop fans, however, they never grow to love the song. Two weeks later, it peaks at No. 50 on Country Airplay. It drops off the chart for the entire month of May; comes back in early June for two more weeks, peaking at No. 50 again; then permanently disappears from country stations. "Road" never gains a solid country radio foothold.

Billboard never does reevaluate the eligibility of "Old Town Road" for the main chart, Hot Country Songs (i.e., following up its "not enough elements . . . in its current version" statement to *Rolling Stone* in March). If country radio had eventually embraced "Road" in normal rotation, that might've allowed the magazine to welcome it back to the chart—without signaling that it took the addition of a white country veteran to make it eligible. Instead, like "Uptown Funk!" in 2015, which was never permitted to chart R&B, "Old Town Road" will never be an official *Billboard* Hot Country hit—with or without Billy Ray Cyrus—beyond its one accidental week at No. 19.

APRIL 16, 2019: The numbers for the Billy Ray Cyrus remix of "Old Town Road" are in. And they're bigger than anyone—from Columbia, to Cyrus, to Lil Nas X, who in December first wished for this in a tweet—could have imagined. It's the most-streamed song in a week, ever.

Combined, the two versions of the song rack up an unprecedented—and, at this writing, still unbeaten—143 million streams in seven days. This easily beats the all-time one-week streaming record of 116 million, previously held by Drake's 2018 hit "In My Feelings." The sales and radio totals for "Road" surge as well—dollar downloads quintuple to 127,000, and airplay more than doubles, finally making "Road" an all-format Top 40 radio hit.

Though *Billboard* does not break down streaming, sales, and airplay ratios for the two mixes, it does reveal that the bulk of the week's activity was for the remix. This is evident on the Hot 100—as of the week ending April 20, 2019, Cyrus's name is added to the chart entry (where it will remain, permanently, for the rest of the song's run; the remix is now considered the flagship). "Old Town Road" by Lil Nas X featuring Billy Ray Cyrus thus becomes Cyrus's first No. 1 pop single, beating his prior Hot 100 peak of No. 4 with "Achy Breaky Heart," twenty-seven years earlier.

You really *can't* question God's plan.

APRIL 17, 2019: A *Rolling Stone* follow-up by Elias Leight confirms that the *Billboard*/Nashville contretemps was the X factor that made "Old Town Road" a blockbuster with people who pay little attention to social-video apps. "It was a fun little TikTok novelty thing that we didn't think was gonna go all the way," says Orlando, Florida, pop radio programmer Will Calder. "The second it got pulled off the country chart, it got the steam it needed to really become mass-appeal. People who aren't really familiar with the memes are now hearing this thing." Calder tells Leight that his station, WPYO, is now playing "Old Town Road" seventy times a week.

APRIL 29, 2019: Lil Nas X and Billy Ray Cyrus make their joint live debut in Indio, California, to perform "Old Town Road" at the Stagecoach Festival, Coachella's country-showcasing sister festival. The pair with America's No. 1 song—for a month now—are there as guests of Thomas Wesley Pentz, better known as Diplo. The electronic dance music DJ famed for hits with M.I.A., Skrillex, Justin Bieber, and Major Lazer is now dabbling in country music under his new persona, Thomas Wesley. At his Stagecoach live set at the Palomino Tent, Diplo uses the occasion of Nas's and Cyrus's visit to premiere his own remix of "Old Town Road." Diplo's reimagining of the track is a solid but not revelatory overhaul, mostly boosting its tempo to a racing pulse. But it is something new for Lil Nas X's song: a true remix (not just an added verse).

This will not be the last time "Road" is remixed during its run for the record books. Data-wise, Diplo's remix matters, because per *Billboard* rules, its streams will be combined with both Nas's original version and Billy Ray's reboot. *Billboard* will later reveal that the song's chart performance is only "assisted slightly" by the Diplo remix—but every little bit of data helps, as Lil Nas X is about to face his first major chart challenger.

MAY 6, 2019: Taylor Swift's "ME!"—the peppy, perky first single from her forthcoming album *Lover*—arrives with a supporting vocal from Panic! at the Disco's Brendon Urie and a wave of prerelease hype. Anticipation is so high that, at the end of April, "ME!" sneaks onto the Hot 100 early, at No. 100, based on just three days of radio airplay. When a full week of streams and sales are collected, the song is expected to slingshot to the top of the Hot 100.

When *Billboard* reveals the new Hot 100 on May 6, "ME!" does indeed vault, from No. 100 to . . . No. 2. Standing in Swift's and Urie's way is "Old Town Road." It's the first of a half dozen new challengers Lil Nas X and Billy Ray Cyrus will fend off from the No. 1 spot during the song's epic run. Such as . . .

MAY 13, 2019: Gen-Z heartthrob Shawn Mendes crashes in at No. 2 in his first week with his initial bid for Song of Summer '19 dominance, "If I Can't Have You." And LNX and BRC easily swat Mendes away for the week ending May 20.

The resilience of "Old Town Road" to this point has been remarkable. Through April and May, its digital consumption has held steady while terrestrial airplay catches up; by mid-May, "Road" has the country's fourth-largest radio audience. But overwhelmingly, it is streaming that is fueling the song's dominance, as "Road" continues to rack up more than 100 million US streams a week, typically two to three times the streams of the second-place hit. (The week in early April the Billy Ray remix dropped, "Road"'s streams were nearly *eight* times that of its nearest contender.) To an extent, "Road" has been achieving these streaming totals with one hand tied behind its back—there has been no glossy music video all this time, only Nas's self-made compilation of *Red Dead Redemption 2* footage, and a second version from Columbia with a still of the remix's cover art while the Cyrus version plays. But that's about to change.

MAY 17, 2019: At midnight on a Friday, Columbia releases what it calls the "Official Movie"—a high-budget music video—for "Old Town Road" to YouTube and Vevo. The cinematic pretensions are a justification for the supersizing of the track. At 5:08, the video's running time is nearly twice the duration of the song in its remixed iteration, let alone the original. It opens with Old West–style credits like a Saturday-afternoon matinee; stars Lil Nas X and Cyrus as horse-riding, gun-toting outlaws; includes an elaborate time-travel plot; and features cameos from comedian Chris Rock, rappers Vince Staples and Rico Nasty, recent remixer Diplo, and even two of the song's behind-the-scenes creators: beatmaker YoungKio and Cyrus-verse cowriter Jozzy.

What is oddly touching about the broadly comical clip, directed by veteran hip-hop video creator Charles "Calmatic" Kidd II, is how the story of the creation of the song, as well as its underlying race-and-genre debate, forms the subtext of the video—really, its text. When 1889 cowboy Lil Nas X crash-lands in 2019, he finds himself amid a street's worth of nonplussed Black citizens. Nas's chaps and two-stepping charm the crowd; Vince Staples even drag-races Nas, car versus horse. The clip's most pointed commentary then arrives as Lil Nas X and Cyrus, decked out in their Nudie-style suits, drop in on a small-town bingo hall. "Our rapping hero seems nervous that he will be rejected by the entirely white crowd," Allegra Frank writes for *Vox*. "But with Cyrus by his side, they quickly warm to him . . . Cyrus validates his self-conscious friend when he doubts he'll find acceptance among classical country folks; it's a role similar to the one Cyrus played in real life." (The bingo hall arrival also foreshadows the triumphant entrance a similarly decked-out Lil Nas X will make in that humble elementary school in Mayfield Heights, Ohio, a dozen days hence.)

Media coverage of the video all but ensures the song's ongoing pop-chart dominance and even briefly gets it back on country radio playlists. Calmatic will later win Best Direction at the 2019 MTV Video Music Awards, and the clip will take Best Music Video at the 2020 Grammys.

MAY 18, 2019: One day after the video arrives, Lil Nas X announces that his debut EP (extended play) minialbum, 7, is recorded and will be released a month later. The EP is named simply for its number of songs, though with both versions of "Old Town Road" included its track count is actually eight.

MAY 28, 2019: The day after Memorial Day, *Billboard* announces not only an eighth week at No. 1 for "Old Town Road" but also its highest US streaming numbers (131 million) since the Billy Ray Cyrus mix arrived back in week 2. It's mostly fueled by the premiere of the video, which opened to 5 million views in its first twenty-four hours and well over 50 million in its first week. In the intervening chart week, even before the video data was in, Nas and Cyrus had dispatched another chart contender, the double-team incursion of bro-pals Ed Sheeran and Justin Bieber with their summery confection "I Don't Care." As a new Hot 100 dated June 1 is announced, Sheeran and Bieber hold at No. 2, their hit even more distant from the video-fortified "Road."

JUNE 3, 2019: As *Billboard* announces a ninth week at No. 1 for "Old Town Road," an interesting challenger is emerging: Billie Eilish, whose album *When We All Fall Asleep, Where Do We Go?* is now in its third week at No. 1 on the Billboard 200 album chart and emerging as 2019's top LP. On the Hot 100, Eilish has been inching up the Top 10 for two months with "Bad Guy," her cunning, sarcastic electro-goth jam. (A key lyric: "Duh.") For the week ending June 8, "Bad Guy" rises to No. 2, a promising move but something of a mirage, as *Billboard* later reveals that "Road" has a three-to-one chart points advantage over "Guy" this week. The signature hit by the seventeen-year-old Eilish will wind up holding the No. 2 slot for nine weeks through most of the summer, settling in for a long, mellow, passive-aggressive battle with her fellow Gen-Z icon.

JUNE 15, 2019: "7 DROPS ON JUNE 21ST!!" tweets the excitable young man with the top song in the country for a tenth week. In the tweet, Lil Nas X reveals the glossy cover art for his 7 EP, and there's a detail in the drawing he wants observant fans to notice.

As a quarter moon glows overhead, a horse-riding Nas—a cowboy hat on his head, an electric guitar strapped over his shoulder, his back to the viewer—is emerging from a valley and gazing at a shining city in the distance. The latticework on many of the buildings sports self-referential *X*'s, and a moonbeam lights a path through the hills surrounding horse and rider, toward the city.

And . . . toward the right, out in front, one building stands out for its color scheme: a rainbow.

From the birth of rock n' roll, in the flamboyant but self-abnegating personage of Little Richard on down, pop music's relationship to LGBTQ+ identity has been deep, undeniable, and tortured. The story of Lil Nas X—born less than nine months before the new millennium; entering adolescence in the Obama era of greater-than-ever US acceptance of gay, trans, and pansexual identity and freedom for LGBTQ+ persons; yet also struggling with self-hatred deep into his teens—shows both how far American culture has come and how very far we have left to go.

Asked in the fall of 2019, a few months after the peak of his crazy year, by CBS newscaster Gayle King if he'd always known he was gay, Montero Hill said, "Yeah—definitely. I knew. Um . . . especially like, around my teenage years, you know. I was like, praying, praying, praying."

"What were you praying for?" King asked.

"That it was, like, a phase."

"That it would go away."

"Yeah, that it would go away."

Seven years earlier, in May 2012, I wrote a *Village Voice* feature examining the chart history of LGBTQ+-identified artists, spurred by the impending release of a new album by *American Idol* finalist–turned–pop/rock star Adam Lambert. I concluded that there had never been, to that date, a No. 1 album by an out gay artist. In other words, every gay or lesbian performer who'd topped the Billboard 200 chart, either solo or with a group, had done so while at least partially closeted. These included, in alphabetical order, Clay Aiken from *American Idol*, Lance Bass of *NSYNC, Elton John, Janis Ian, Jonathan Knight of New Kids on the Block, Ricky Martin, Freddie Mercury of Queen, George Michael (both with Wham! and solo), and Michael Stipe of R.E.M. (Such famed queer artists as Boy George, k.d. lang, and Melissa Etheridge had no chart-topping LPs.) My readers countered with two examples of chart-topping, largely straight-identified bisexuals: Lady Gaga, who'd just scored a No. 1 LP with *Born This Way* in 2011; and Billie Joe Armstrong of Green Day, which had topped the chart in the '00s with *American Idiot* and a follow-up. Even with these partial exceptions—and an asterisk for Stipe, who was beginning to talk more openly about his sexuality in 1994 when R.E.M. scored its second No. 1 LP, *Monster*—the list of queer chart-toppers was exceedingly small.

I did my study in light of Lambert, who, while on *Idol* in 2009, was closeted (but with a coy wink) and then immediately came out to *Rolling Stone* after completing the competition. (Lambert finished second on *Idol* to straight performer Kris Allen.) When *Trespassing*, Lambert's second LP, debuted atop the Billboard 200 in 2012, he became the first indisputably out gay person with America's No. 1 album.

As for the Hot 100, the list of out gay acts with No. 1 songs was also scant. By 2012, I counted only eight No. 1s—out of more than a thousand in the chart's history—by just four artists. Avowed bisexuals David Bowie and Lady Gaga scored five of them—two by Bowie ("Fame," 1975, and "Let's Dance," 1983) and three by Gaga ("Just Dance" and "Poker Face," 2009, and "Born This Way," 2011). Elton John, after coming fully out in the '90s, scored his last two No. 1s, "Don't Let the Sun Go Down on Me," a 1992 live duet with a still-closeted George Michael, and the Princess Diana eulogy "Candle in the Wind 1997." And Richard Fairbrass, a member of Right Said Fred, took "I'm Too Sexy" to the top in 1992, coincidentally the week after John's and Michael's "Sun" duet.

In the decade since my initial study—during the '10s, as a questioning Montero Hill entered his teenage years—acceptance within the music industry most certainly improved, and there were more chart victories by LGBTQ+ acts, if still a relatively small number. Queer-identified artists Rostam Batmanglij of Vampire Weekend, Brittany Howard of Alabama Shakes, Frank Ocean, Halsey, and Tyler, the Creator scored No. 1 albums during the '10s;

and on the Hot 100, Janelle Monáe, Halsey, and Gaga scored chart-topping singles. But for other openly gay artists like dance-pop star Troye Sivan or Neon Trees front man Tyler Glenn, the commercial picture was more mixed.

For the young Montero Hill, the most significant coming-out among these artists was Frank Ocean. The alternative-R&B singer—who, along with Tyler, the Creator, was a former member of turn-of-the-'10s hip-hop collective Odd Future—published a Tumblr post on July 4, 2012, revealing a prior, unrequited relationship with a man at age nineteen. "I don't know what happens now, and that's alright," Ocean wrote. "I don't have any secrets I need kept anymore . . . I feel like a free man." Despite concern that the worlds of R&B and hip-hop were suffused with homophobia, Ocean's revelation was met largely with support, and his career was not negatively affected in any discernible way. Less than a month after the Tumblr post, Ocean's *Channel Orange* debuted at No. 2 on the Billboard 200; the following year it went gold and won a Grammy Award. His follow-up album *Blond* debuted at No. 1 in 2016.

When Lil Nas X was asked in 2020 by Apple Music DJ Zane Lowe how Frank Ocean factored into his life, he replied, "I think artists like Frank, in general, and, like, Tyler [the Creator] and whatever, they made it easier for me to be where I am, comfortably."

But in June 2019—in the middle of Pride Month, while holding down the No. 1 song in America—Montero Hill was still weighing how comfortable he was revealing himself.

"It's not like everybody is, like, messing with *me* now," Lil Nas X would later tell Gayle King. "Somebody who's, like, listening to me in school right now, it's like, 'You're gay, 'cuz you're listening to him.' So it's like, there's still a lot to be done, of course."

JUNE 23, 2019: Two days after the 7 EP drops, and as "Old Town Road" completes its eleventh week at No. 1, Lil Nas X and Billy Ray Cyrus perform their smash onstage at the 2019 BET Awards in Los Angeles. Leading off with a pretaped bit where the pair ride horses past the Staples Center, they enter the Microsoft Theater fully decked out in their hats and fringed outfits, Lil Nas X looking especially flamboyant in canary yellow, shirtless under an open jacket. They walk out onto a saloon-themed stage to an army of two-stepping dancers in hats, denim, and boots, plus a live band complete with a brass section. The BET audience—both fans and celebrities, from Cardi B to John Legend—knows every word, and the only line they sing with more brio than the chorus is the hip-hop–derived refrain, "Can't nobody tell me *nothiiiiin'.*"

JUNE 24, 2019: *Billboard* announces the new Hot 100, and Lil Nas X has fended off a repeat challenger. For the week ending June 29, Taylor Swift returns with another No. 2 hit, "You Need to Calm Down." Despite strong download sales, the streams and initial airplay for "Calm" fall short, and Swift debuts and peaks in the runner-up slot behind "Old Town Road." Swift's bubbly electropop single doubles as an antihatred anthem. Supported by a video filled with LGBTQ+ celebrities—from Adam Lambert to Laverne Cox, Ellen DeGeneres to RuPaul—"Calm" is intended by the straight Swift as a message of solidarity, its release specifically timed for Pride Month. Lil Nas X is about to make his own contribution to that discourse.

JUNE 30, 2019: "deadass thought i made it obvious"

With that tweet, less than five hours before the end of Pride Month, Lil Nas X makes his sexual identity official. The post includes a cropped close-up of the rainbow building from the cover of the 7 EP. And it follows, by just a couple of hours, a tweet of an animated video for "C7osure," a deep cut from the mini-album: "some of y'all already know," Nas writes, "some of y'all don't care, some of y'all not gone fwm [going to fuck with me] no more. but before this month ends i want y'all to listen closely to c7osure"—with emoji of a rainbow and stars. The song's lyrics:

> *Ain't no more actin', man*
> *That forecast say I should just let me grow*
> *No more red light for me, baby*
> *Only green, I gotta go*
> *Pack my past up in the back*
> *Oh, let my future take a hold*
> *This is what I gotta do*
> *Can't be regrettin' when I'm old*

It's a new first for Lil Nas X, and chart history: a coming-out by the artist with the current No. 1 song in America. It shows remarkable fearlessness by a twenty-year-old on only his debut single.

The news is greeted, and digested, by the media during the week of July 1. "Wait, Did Lil Nas X Just Come Out?" reads the headline from online magazine *Pride*. The *New York Times* reports that "Lil Nas X's tweets were met with an outpouring of support from fans online, many of them promising to spring to his defense if he became a target because of his sexuality." Montero accepts congratulatory tweets and Instagram comments, ranging from Diplo to NBA star Dwyane Wade to South Bend, Indiana, mayor and presidential candidate Pete Buttigieg.

For the week ending July 6, "Old Town Road" is in its thirteenth week at No. 1. The true test will come a week later, when the impact of Montero Hill's revelation manifests in *Billboard*'s math.

JULY 8, 2019: And there is essentially no falloff, as "Old Town Road" holds for a fourteenth week, its streams slightly up, its downloads and airplay slightly down ("Road" had peaked at radio in early June, making the later Pride revelation a nonevent). America is still rooting for Lil Nas X.

The week of the revelation, Lil Nas X held off yet another repeat challenger, as Shawn Mendes debuts at No. 2 a second time, with "Señorita," his duet with Camila Cabello. "Old Town Road" is now three weeks away from setting the all-time record for No. 1 longevity (sixteen weeks), jointly held by Mariah Carey and Boyz II Men's "One Sweet Day" and Luis Fonsi, Daddy Yankee, and Justin Bieber's "Despacito." As "Señorita" pulls back, Billie Eilish returns to No. 2 with "Bad Guy." It will prove to be Lil Nas X's most formidable challenger, especially when Eilish and Nas each bring in backup. Eilish's gambit even involves the guy who made a chart-topper out of "Despacito."

JULY 11, 2019: As a tween, Billie Eilish idolized Justin Bieber. Now, as the possessor of 2019's hottest album and longest-running No. 2 single, she welcomes him as a guest on that song's first-ever remix. Reinforcing her motivation for the reboot, the single's cover art is a photo of a younger Eilish in a princess dress, her bedroom walls plastered with Bieber posters.

Over the prior four years, Justin Bieber had matured from teen idol into the ultimate hitmaking secret weapon. He turned songs as varying as Skrillex and Diplo's "Where Are Ü Now," DJ Khaled's "I'm the One," and, of course, "Despacito" into monster hits. Now he's providing a third-act plot twist to Billie Eilish's quest to overtake Lil Nas X. Critics are, by and large, not impressed with Bieber's tacked-on verse—typical of the reviews is *Stereogum*'s, in which Chris DeVille calls Bieber "entirely out of place . . . he basically ruins a great song." But that will prove immaterial, if his "Belieber" army downloads and streams "Bad Guy" version 2.0 and takes it the last mile.

As it happens, Lil Nas X has been ready for this eventuality and calls in his own reinforcements.

JULY 12, 2019: Columbia releases the third remix (and fourth official version) of "Old Town Road," retaining Billy Ray Cyrus's vocals and piling in new verses from Jeffery Lamar Williams, better known as Young Thug—originator of the country-trap sound on 2017's *Beautiful Thugger Girls*—and a twelve-year-old named

Mason Ramsey. The year before, Ramsey starred in a viral video yodeling Hank Williams's classic "Lovesick Blues" at a Walmart. Now renowned as the "Yodeling Kid," Ramsey has signed a recording contract and even scored a Hot Country chart hit with "Famous." In the country cosmos of 2019, Ramsey is about as genre-authentic as Billy Ray Cyrus.

The remix is muddled but has meme-worthy highlights. Thug reprises his "Yee-haw!" from "Family Don't Matter," and Ramsey gets the best new lyrics: "Hop up in my Razor . . . If you ain't got no giddee-up, then giddee out my way." (Given Lil Nas X's huge prepubescent fan base, Ramsey's Razor scooter reference is savvy fan service.) Thug's and Ramsey's names are never added to the chart entry for "Old Town Road," because their mix does not account for the bulk of the song's points (unlike the original Cyrus remix, which remains the overwhelming radio and streaming favorite).

Nonetheless, arriving twenty-four hours after the Bieber-fied "Bad Guy," this four-dude "Road" is a shrewd insurance policy. Lil Nas X even stakes their bid further by issuing an animated video for the remix depicting a four-cowboy raid on Area 51—Nas leveraging yet another online meme. Game on.

JULY 22, 2019: After its first full week of chart activity, the new version of "Bad Guy" sees a 40 percent gain in streams and a 64 percent gain in downloads—Bieber's hitmaking pixie dust working its magic again. And . . . it's not enough: "Bad Guy" holds at No. 2.

Billboard reveals that the Thug/Ramsey remix didn't give "Old Town Road" as big of a bump as Bieber's version gave Eilish's hit, but "Road" still has a 1.3-to-1 points lead over "Bad Guy." Now in its sixteenth week at No. 1, "Road" has tied the record held by Mariah/Boyz and Fonsi/Daddy/Bieber. The all-time record is his to lose.

JULY 24, 2019: As one more insurance policy during its final lap, Lil Nas X issues the last of the official "Old Town Road" remixes, and the only one not to feature vocals from Billy Ray Cyrus. Subtitled "Seoul Town Road," this version features South Korean rapper RM ("Rap Monster") of K-pop sensations BTS. RM raps in English and sings the opening chorus in Cyrus's place.

The reboots have come so fast and furious that the interwebs are starting to expect them and even poke some good-natured fun at Lil Nas X ("Search Party Seeks Lil Nas X after No New 'Old Town Road' Remixes in over 48 Hours," reads a headline at comedy website *The Hard Times*). In a tweet, Lil Nas X claims the K-pop remix is the "last one i PROMISSEE." But even that's not guaranteed—a remix with rap titan Lil Wayne, ultimately shelved, has already leaked.

JULY 29, 2019: *Billboard* makes it official. For the week ending August 3, "Old Town Road" is in its seventeenth week atop the Hot 100—the longest-running No. 1 single in the chart's history. Two days later, Mariah Carey's official Twitter account sends out a congratulatory tweet, with a Photoshopped image of Carey literally passing a torch to Montero Hill in his canary-yellow cowboy outfit: "Sending love & congrats to @LilNasX on breaking one of the longest running records in music history! We've been blessed to hold this record with a song that means a great deal to @BoyzIIMen and myself and has touched so many. Keep living your best life!"

Lil Nas X and Billy Ray Cyrus will hold the top of the Hot 100 for an eighteenth and a nineteenth week. Not until the third week of August does *Billboard* announce that Billie Eilish's "Bad Guy," after a record nine weeks at No. 2, finally replaces "Old Town Road" at No. 1. As it happens, the Justin Bieber remix is long faded from streaming services; Eilish's original mix is what ultimately rings the bell.

"Old Town Road" will ride the Hot 100 another five months, finally falling off the Hot 100 after forty-five weeks. The Recording Industry Association of America will eventually certify the single "14-times platinum," the highest certification total for any digital-era single.

AUGUST 15, 2019: Gracing the cover of *Time* magazine in a cherry-red suit, a red hat to match, and a pair of cow-print boots, Montero Lamar Hill stands tall and proud next to the headline, "It's His Country: The Wild Ride of Lil Nas X."

The cover package includes a searching opinion piece, coauthored by progressive country star Tim McGraw and Chattanooga–based historian Jon Meacham, on the lack of racial and ethnic diversity in country music. "Country is in the midst of a renewed debate over the nature of its sound and the related question of who counts as part of its club," they write. "The answer, much like the music itself, is more complicated than even its fans tend to realize."

In the lead interview, conducted once again by *Time*'s Andrew Chow, Lil Nas X discusses the series of events that led him to come out in June ("I never would have done that if I wasn't, in a way, pushed by the universe"). He is equally cosmic in his estimation of everything that's happened to him in the last year—during which he discovered a banjo-based beat by a Dutch kid, recorded some intentionally comical lyrics, sparked the biggest social meme *and* cultural movement of the year, and took the country (and Country) by storm. In the six months after *Time*'s story, Lil Nas X's Frankenstein's monster of a song will take home two Grammys, an American Music Award, two MTV VMAs, Nickelodeon Kids' Choice and Teen Choice prizes, two BET Hip-Hop Awards, and the Country Music Association's Musical Event of the Year prize.

"Everything lined up for this moment to take me to this place," Montero Hill tells Andrew Chow. "Not to sound self-centered, but it feels like I'm chosen, in a way, to do this stuff."

Epilogue
PRIDE 'til I Can't No More

How Lil Nas X Became a Multihit Wonder

"OLD TOWN ROAD" WAS SUCH a singular phenomenon, it provided no roadmap for how anyone or anything could follow it up. Would it have any legacy at all? Hearteningly, it has—albeit a profoundly unpredictable one.

"Road" signaled a new wave of Black crossover in country music. Before 2019 was even over, Blanco Brown bettered Lil Nas X by taking his line-dance instructional song "The Git Up" to No. 44 on the Country Airplay chart and No. 1 on Hot Country Songs. Remarkably, *Billboard* allowed this country-trap novelty track onto that chart, as it was more readily embraced by the Nashville establishment. In 2020, the magazine also permitted Breland's trappier and twangier "My Truck" onto Hot Country Songs, where it hit No. 26. A remix featuring country stalwart Sam Hunt helped, but the New Jersey–born Breland got the single onto the chart by himself. Even more traditionally minded Black country acts felt freer to try pop and hip-hop-leaning tracks, like Kane Brown, whose 2021 hit "Memory," a collaboration with alt-R&B singer Blackbear, scored little Country airplay but was allowed onto Hot Country Songs anyway, where it peaked at No. 9. You might say Lil Nas X died at Country radio so others might live.

And what about Montero Lamar Hill himself? In the end, Lil Nas X did not turn out to be a country artist. He would never tangle with Nashville again, or try to make *Billboard*'s Country charts. He did feint in that direction at first, between the cowboy iconography on his 7 EP and such deep cuts on the minialbum as "Rodeo." In early 2021, Nas even released a children's book, *C Is for Country*, featuring a colorful guitar-wielding, horse-riding cowboy on the cover. Nas was inspired to write the early reader by the way his nieces and nephews keyed into his cowboy persona, and the way those Lander Elementary School kids reacted in that gymnasium.

But Lil Nas X did not turn out to be a kiddie artist. Or, for that matter, a timid one.

That was made clear by "Montero (Call Me by Your Name)," his 2021 single. Fiendishly catchy and impossible to pigeonhole, "Montero" opens with a Tex-Mex–style guitar, quickly shifts to a syncopated Latin-style beat—one critic aptly labeled it "flamenco and reggaeton dipped in pop"—then shifts again to a technopop-like chorus in which Nas croons like an automaton, and finally pivots toward a romantic bridge with aching Gen Z–style vocals. The song is decidedly adult and openly queer, depicting a lustful relationship with a male partner: "You live in the dark, boy, I cannot pretend." Its music video, an homage to Hieronymus Bosch's *Garden of Earthly Delights*, depicted Nas descending into hell, twerking for Satan and having sex with the demon before killing him and assuming his infernal throne. Nas would go on to further flaunt his uncloseted status, kissing men on awards shows and continuing to play with camp in his costumes and his lyrics. Having tiptoed out of the closet in 2019, Lil Nas X became pop's proudest, most unguarded LGBTQ+ icon.

Lil Nas X also did not, contrary to early expectations, become a one-hit wonder. While in 2019 his other singles fell well short of the No. 1 spot—only "Panini" managed a brief No. 5 peak—in 2021 Nas made good on his early promise. "Montero" bested "Old Town Road" as a chart phenomenon by not only hitting No. 1 but *entering* the Hot 100 on top. As ever, the former Nicki Minaj superfan made expert use of digital media, from Twitter to TikTok to Roblox, to promote his wares. He posted pro-gay messages, picked playful fights with conservative critics, and even promoted the sale of limited-edition, "Montero"-branded "Satan sneakers." A second single, "Industry Baby," made a splash with a music video shot in a prison, with all-male nude drill-team dancers. If a mix of art and commerce is what makes songs hits—not just the content but also the metacontent—Lil Nas X was game to offer layers of meta, refereeing his own discourse. Were we not entertained?

For all that cultural chum, however, Nas's most underrated achievement was becoming a firmly established purveyor of hit music—as in hit songs, not just memes. His 2021 singles were radio smashes: "Montero" spent seven months on *Billboard*'s Radio Songs chart, about two months longer than "Old Town Road" had lasted on pop playlists. Its follow-ups—"Industry Baby" and the '80s-style rock song "That's What I Want"—spent forty-plus weeks apiece on radio playlists, or roughly nine months each. This utterly belied the thumbnail sketch of Lil Nas X, of a dude who savvily surfed internet culture to generate hits. In 2021, radio programmers determined that listeners—across demographics, not just teens—wanted to hear Nas in regular rotation on their radios, where neither clever tweets nor lurid videos made a difference.

....

As of this writing, Lil Nas X is not only a legitimate but also a pre-dominant pop star. That's *pop* as in "popular," but also *pop* as in unconstrained by the bounds of format. Though media outlets persist in calling Nas a "rapper," pop is closest to his core. If he has a genre, it's "internet."

This, at last, may be the greatest legacy of "Old Town Road." It dominated the charts but also hacked the formula, queering—literally and figuratively—the very definition of genre and resetting the parameters by which we measure what a hit is. By spending nineteen weeks atop the Hot 100, "Old Town Road" both reinforced that chart's cultural value and rebooted how it works. It proved that Montero Hill's digital-first, populist instincts were fundamentally correct.

Can't nobody tell him nothin'.

ACKNOWLEDGMENTS

This book's existence is owed to Joshua Clover and Emily Lordi. At the annual Pop Conference in Seattle back in April 2019, Lil Nas X's "Old Town Road" first went to No. 1, and I broke from the conference for a day to write about it for my *Slate* series "Why Is This Song No. 1?" When I returned, Joshua approached me to compliment the article, which was hugely gratifying, as we'd previously only admired each other's work from afar. This paid dividends more than a year later, when he and Emily were choosing authors to recommend for the Singles series. It was Emily who approached me with the idea to do a book on "Old Town Road." My schedule is such that I need persuading to take on projects I know will ultimately be good for me, and Emily—with her brilliant mind, sterling scholarship, and ebullient enthusiasm—can probably talk me into anything. Throughout this book's genesis, Joshua and Emily have served as sherpas through the academy, readers of chapters, cheerleaders when I didn't know if I would finish, and all-around inspirations. I quite literally can't thank them enough.

I am also grateful to Ken Wissoker, who has been endlessly encouraging both before I started this book and as it took shape, and everyone on the Duke University Press team.

This is my first book in twenty years. When I published the last one, I was mostly a record reviewer and blogger who tried to sneak *Billboard* chart references into my reviews. The wholesale shift in my career toward writing critically about the charts as a full-time pursuit began in 2007, and I owe it to Maura Johnston, who gave me my first chart column at *Idolator*, took me with her to the *Village Voice*, has given me more writing opportunities than I can count, and has never stopped making me feel valued as a writer and a friend. I have called Maura my guardian angel.

Another thing that happened in those intervening two decades was the publication of *Let's Talk about Love* by my *Slate* colleague Carl Wilson. His seminal installment in the 33⅓ book series provided a model for *Old Town Road* in its ingenious use of a primary musical artifact as a springboard to a larger dissection of how we measure our culture. Carl continues to inspire me.

Other benevolent spirits and friends of my writing have included Chris Berube, Tom Breihan, Rachel Brodsky, Franklin Bruno, Jon Caramanica, David Cantwell, Raymond Cummings, Phil Dellio, Steacy Easton, Gavin Edwards, Stephen Thomas Erlewine, Tom Ewing, Ben Frisch, Jeff Gage, Jacob Ganz, Sarah Grant, David Haglund, Jack Hamilton, Charlie Harding, Aisha Harris, Keith Harris, Eric Harvey, Rob Harvilla, Jewly Hight, Jessica Hopper, "Hollywood" Steve Huey, Charles Hughes, Thomas Inskeep, Rich Juzwiak, Jason King, Mara Kuge, Josh Langhoff, Jenn Lena, Steve Lickteig, Alan Light, Amy Linden, Dorian Lynskey, Kim Mack, Lori Majewski, Jill Mapes, Michaelangelo Matos, Erin MacLeod, Geoff Mayfield, Stephen Metcalf, Wesley Morris, Paul Myers, Chris O'Leary, Nate Patrin, Mike Pesca, Amanda Petrusich, Ann Powers, Ned Raggett, Caryn Rose, Jody Rosen, Sean Ross, Asha Saluja, Barry Shank, Rob Sheffield, Nate Sloan, Danyel Smith, Jay Smooth, Alfred Soto, Dana Stevens, Karen Tongson, Julia Turner, Andrew Unterberger, Oliver Wang, Matt Wardlaw, Eric Weisbard, Forrest Wickman, Douglas Wolk, Scott Woods, Annie Zaleski, Andy Zax, and Lindsay Zoladz. At various moments—whether or not you knew that I needed it—you have inspired me and made me feel like my life's project had value.

This book was completed during a challenging year in my personal life. I am deeply grateful to Euny Hong for making me feel appreciated, admired, and capable again. I was also fortified by the stalwart friendship of Danielle Pelfrey Duryea—my benevolent spirit since college—and Peter and Courtney Marsh and their wonderful daughters, who treated me like family at a time when a surrogate family was what I needed. And, of course, I remain thankful for my parents and my sister Catherine (Tc'cho) for loving me unconditionally and always having my back.

Finally, though I was a stepfather for a scant few years, the children I was fortunate to help raise gave me a window into Gen-Z culture that immeasurably enriched my understanding of the music I wrote about. That included "Old Town Road" and its memeability. I will always think of Anna and Loki when I think of that song. May you both ride 'til you can't no more.

BIBLIOGRAPHY

Ahlgrim, Callie. "Billy Ray Cyrus Says Lil Nas X Only Knew He Made Country Music because of 'Hannah Montana.'" *Business Insider*, January 31, 2020.

Aku, Timmhotep. "Brooklyn Rapper Bobby Shmurda Goes from Vine Star to Major-Label Player." *Billboard*, August 26, 2014.

Asker, Jim. "Chart Rewind: In 1962, Ray Charles' 'Stop' Started Its No. 1 Hot 100 Run." *Billboard*, June 2, 2022.

Atwood, Brett. "The History of the Music Industry's First-Ever Digital Single for Sale, 20 Years after Its Release." *Billboard*, September 13, 2017.

Bastone, Nick. "TikTok Was the Most-Downloaded App in the US in September." *Business Insider*, November 2, 2018.

Battan, Carrie. "'Old Town Road' and the Overdue Death of Genre." *New Yorker*, April 8, 2019.

Bronson, Fred. *The Billboard Book of Number 1 Hits*. New York: Billboard Books, 2003.

Burns, Ken. *Country Music* (miniseries). PBS, 2019.

Carmichael, Rodney. "Wrangler on His Booty: Lil Nas X on the Making and the Magic of 'Old Town Road.'" *NPR Music*, April 10, 2019.

Chow, Andrew R. "Lil Nas X Talks 'Old Town Road' and the Billboard Controversy." *Time*, April 5, 2019.

Chow, Andrew R. "Inside Lil Nas X's Record-Breaking, Culture-Changing Summer." *Time*, August 15, 2019.

Coroneos, Kyle ("Trigger"). "Billboard Must Remove Lil Nas X's 'Old Town Road' from Country Chart." *Saving Country Music* (blog), March 23, 2019.

Coscarelli, Joe. "'Old Town Road': See How Memes and Controversy Took Lil Nas X to the Top of the Charts." *New York Times*, May 10, 2019.

Cuby, Michael. "Lil Nas X Praised Frank Ocean and Tyler, the Creator for Making It Easier for Queer Artists." *Them*, December 5, 2020.

DeVille, Chris. "Justin Bieber Hops on Billie Eilish's 'Bad Guy.'" *Stereogum*, July 11, 2019.

Düren, Breanne. "Interview with Steve Bursky, Manager at Foundations for Owl City." *Hit Quarters*, July 11, 2011.

Eells, Josh. "Lil Nas X: Ballad of a Hip-Hop Cowboy." *Rolling Stone*, May 20, 2019.

Ermac, Raffy. "Wait, Did Lil Nas X Just Come Out?" *Pride*, June 30, 2019.

Feldman, Brian, Dee Lockett, et al. "The 23 Most Important Vines of All Time." *Vulture*, October 28, 2016.

Frank, Allegra. "Lil Nas X's 'Old Town Road' Is a Banger. But Is It Country? Depends on Whom You Ask." *Vox*, April 5, 2019.

Frank, Allegra. "Lil Nas X's 'Old Town Road' Music Video Is a Time-Traveling Western." *Vox*, May 17, 2019.

Ghosh, Devarati. "The Meaningless Florida-Georgia Line *Billboard* Country Songs Record: Who Really Has the Biggest Country Hit?" *MJ's Big Blog*, August 2, 2013.

Gracie, Bianca. "TLC's 'FanMail' Turns 20: A Track-by-Track Retrospective with the Girl Group and Behind-the-Scenes Collaborators." *Billboard*, February 22, 2019.

Guralnick, Peter. "What'd He Say!" *Washington Post*, March 13, 1983.

Haider, Shuja. "The Invention of Twang." *The Believer*, August 1, 2019.

Hong, Euny. *The Birth of Korean Cool: How One Nation Is Conquering the World through Pop Culture*. New York: Picador, 2014.

Hughes, Charles. *Country Soul: Making Music and Making Race in the American South*. Chapel Hill: University of North Carolina Press, 2015.

Hughes, Jazmine. "The Subversive Joy of Lil Nas X's Gay Pop Stardom." *New York Times Magazine*, July 7, 2021.

Jacobs, Julia. "Lil Nas X Comes Out on Last Day of Pride Month." *New York Times*, July 1, 2019.

Jones, Jonathan. "*Red Dead Redemption 2* Critiques White History for an Audience Susceptible to Alt-Right Ideology." *Slate*, February 4, 2019.

Kim, Michelle Hyun. "How Solange and Mitski Reconsider Who Can Be the Cowboy." *Pitchfork*, March 21, 2019.

King, Gayle. "Lil Nas X Opens Up about the Difficulties of Coming Out: 'We Still Have a Long Way to Go.'" CBS News, September 30, 2019.

King, Gayle. "Lil Nas X Takes Gayle King inside the Studio Where He Recorded 'Old Town Road.'" CBS News, September 30, 2019.

Kunzru, Hari. "That Ain't Country." *Into the Zone* (podcast), September 3, 2020.

Lamarre, Carl. "'Old Town Road' Producer YoungKio on How Lil Nas X's Song Came to Life." *Billboard*, March 28, 2019.

Lawrence, Keith. "Arnold Shultz: The Greatest (?) Guitar Picker's Life Ended before Promise Realized." IBMA Foundation website, October 22, 2020.

Leight, Elias. "Lil Nas X's 'Old Town Road' Was a Country Hit. Then Country Changed Its Mind." *Rolling Stone*, March 26, 2019.

Leight, Elias. "Fueled by Controversy, Lil Nas X's 'Old Town Road' Is on a Record-Breaking Run." *Rolling Stone*, April 17, 2019.

Lewis, Randy. "Record Producer Was Godfather of R&B." *Los Angeles Times*, August 16, 2008.

Lewry, Fraser. "The Day Aerosmith Changed the Internet as We Know It." *Classic Rock*, June 27, 2022.

Lockett, Dee. "Everything You Need to Know about the 'Shmoney Dance.'" *Slate*, July 15, 2014.

Martin, Rachel. "Lil Nas X, Country Music's Unlikely Son, Sparks Conversation on Genre and Race." KCUR-NPR Kansas City, May 23, 2019.

McGraw, Tim, and Jon Meacham. "Country Music Should Be Political. After All, It Always Has Been." *Time*, August 15, 2019.

McKinley, James C., Jr. "*Billboard*'s Changes to Charts Draw Fire." *New York Times*, October 26, 2012.

McKinney, Kelsey. "A Hit Song Is Usually 3 to 5 Minutes Long. Here's Why." *Vox*, January 30, 2015.

Nodjimbadem, Katie. "The Lesser-Known History of African-American Cowboys." *Smithsonian*, February 13, 2017.

Pearce, Sheldon. "How Lil Nas X's 'Old Town Road' Became a Lightning Rod for Race, the Charts, and Country Music." *Pitchfork*, April 1, 2019.

Pecknold, Diane. *Hidden in the Mix: The African American Presence in Country Music*. Durham, NC: Duke University Press, 2013.

Petrusich, Amanda. "Lil Nas X Is the Sound of the Internet, Somehow." *New Yorker*, June 24, 2019.

Petrusich, Amanda. "Genre Is Disappearing. What Comes Next?" *New Yorker*, March 8, 2021.

Reese, Ashley. "What Everyone Is Getting Wrong about the 'Yee Haw Agenda,' according to Bri Malandro, the Woman Who Coined the Term." *Jezebel*, March 27, 2019.

Royster, Francesca T. *Black Country Music: Listening for Revolutions*. Austin: University of Texas Press, 2022.

Scott, Jason. "*Billboard*, Stop the Use of Multi-format Airplay in Determining 'Hit' Country, R&B, Rock Songs." Change.org, October 12, 2012.

Sisario, Ben. "Lil Nas X Added Billy Ray Cyrus to 'Old Town Road.' Is It Country Enough for *Billboard* Now?" *New York Times*, April 5, 2019.

Solomon, Matt. "How Lonely Island Launched YouTube." *Cracked*, August 3, 2022.

Stopera, Matt. "40 Sad Portraits of Closed Record Stores." *Buzzfeed*, April 11, 2011.

Strauss, Neil. "Hit Makers Warily Explore the Computer Frontier." *New York Times*, July 6, 1994.

Tingen, Paul. "Inside Track: Lil Nas X ft Billy Ray Cyrus 'Old Town Road.'" *Sound on Sound*, August 2019.

Trust, Gary. "Lil Nas X's 'Old Town Road' Leaps to No. 1 on *Billboard* Hot 100." *Billboard*, April 8, 2019.

Trust, Gary. "Lil Nas X's 'Old Town Road' Debuts on Country Airplay, Driven by Morning Show Spins." *Billboard*, April 9, 2019.

Weisbard, Eric. *Top 40 Democracy: The Rival Mainstreams of American Music*. Chicago: University of Chicago Press, 2014.

Whitburn, Joel. *Top Country Singles 1944–2017*. Menomenee Falls, WI: Record Research, 2018.

Whitburn, Joel. *Top Pop Albums 1955–2016*. Menomenee Falls, WI: Record Research, 2018.

Whitburn, Joel. *Top Pop Singles 1955–2018*. Menomenee Falls, WI: Record Research, 2019.

Whitburn, Joel. *Top R&B Singles 1942–2016*. Menomenee Falls, WI: Record Research, 2017.

Witt, Stephen. *How Music Got Free: A Story of Obsession and Invention*. New York: Penguin, 2016.

Zellner, Xander. "Spurred by a TikTok Meme, Lil Nas X Scores First Hot 100 Hit with 'Old Town Road.'" *Billboard*, March 13, 2019.

Zoladz, Lindsay. "'Old Town Road' Isn't Country or Rap or Even Internet—It's Pure Bliss." *The Ringer*, April 8, 2019.

INDEX